ACKNOWLEDGMENTS

I gratefully acknowledge everyone who has held out a cup of water to someone pursuing their dream.

Dione, my training companion and biggest fan, who reads every chapter as I write them, and kindly notes the misspelled words, thank you.

Mom and Dad, if I become a marathon-runner, you will go to the races and ring cowbells. For I am your little bunny.

Coach Art, for believing in a total novice for no reason but faith and enthusiasm, and showing me the joys of running. Justin and everyone at Endurance House for the gear and support of the sport. Coach Jackie, for just the right amount of ass-kicking at just the right times. Marit and Inner Fire Yoga for sharing the abundance of presence and peace; namaste.

To my fellow creators, for sustaining an environment where projects like this come to life. JPT and Annika, thank you.

To everyone who dreams of a goal worth telling stories about, and to all those who didn't choose the challenges that they bravely endure nonetheless.

Dan Tyler
Madison, 12 December 2012

CONTENTS

Acknowledgments   *iii*

Prologue   *vii*

Part I: A Really Big Race

The Big One   3
Signing Up   6
How to Worry   10
A Year of Training   17
Smiling at the Edge of Consciousness   24
A Year of Prioritizing   30
Race Report: Ironman Wisconsin 2009   36
A Day-long Surprise Party   42
Presence and the Transformation   47

Part II: For Something Greater

Genesis   55
To Find a Team   59
Race Report: Mardi Gras Marathon   63
Some Days you Race, Some Days you Make
Races Happen   70
Essential Input from the Benevolent Observer   74
Becoming a Leader   78
Race Report: San Diego Marathon   83
Taking it Out Into the World   89
Very Hard Things   94
Why Wait?   99

Part III: Tri Therapy

Credit for Character   109

A Tale of Triathlon and Football   115

Race Report: Athens Marathon   122

A Case for Space   128

A Different Kind of Ready   133

Race Report: Ironman Wisconsin 2011   140

The Streak   147

New York City - and Beyond   151

Tri Therapy   155

For Perpetuity   159

PROLOGUE

Friday, 13 August 2010. Madison, Wisconsin.

It's getting darker, and even when I lift my fogged-over yellow safety glasses, I can't see any better. The continuously rolling thunder in the background is gradually transitioning into more discrete crashes in the foreground, where I am standing drenched and filthy. It's hot - like it's been all week - and the rain feels great, even though mosquitoes are winning more than their fair share through my long sleeves and pants. The dense humidity seems to trap me in the pungent cloud of two-cycle engine smoke, and my soggy pants hang on to the sawdust like glue.

I'm cutting up a limb that fell in my neighbor's back yard during a storm that rolled in earlier that day - a big 20-inch branch from a 100-or-more-year-old silver maple. Fortunately, it happened to fall perfectly: away from the house, right between the garage and the power lines, into the narrow sliver of lawn in her back yard. Unfortunately, this older neighbor has lived here in her childhood home by herself since her parents died, and is limited in strength due to a degenerative muscle condition. I have cared for her lawn and yard practically since the day I moved in and we met: why should she pay an impersonal lawn service when I can swing by for a few minutes each time I tend my own yard?

After all, I still have the commercial-sized mower I bought when I was the high school kid on the block who started his own business cutting the neighbors' lawns. My little business grew to include tending the community grounds... it was quite an endeavor by the time I left it to go to college. Today, I'd be selfish to confine a 14-horsepower 48-inch hydrostatic zero-turn walk-behind mower to a single quarter-acre lot. And isn't that what being part of a community is all about - neighbors helping each other? It isn't even hard. It would take my neighbor a lot of time, effort, or money to do the work herself, but it's practically incidental for me. As a matter of fact, it's quite fun.

There's nothing like chain sawing. Oh man. However, on a quarter-acre lot shaded by precisely two 100-or-more-year-old silver maples, the occasion to practice it is rare, and indeed usually unwelcome. So the limb coming down in the backyard next door - distress in a yard under my care - was a veritable call to arms! I can't tell you what else might have been on my task list that evening, it all went out of my head; there was only one project needing attention just then. My mission was to get started and make as much progress as I could before twilight, so the neighbor could feel comfortable that I was taking care of her yard, and taking care of her.

Now I'm here in the thick of it, heated up, soaking wet, and on a roll. There's already order to the job - a pile for limbs and a pile for logs. There's safety in approaching each limb with the knowledge from all the other limbs I've cut over the years; there's immediate progress with each cut that clears the path to the next cut ahead. I must not stop. It's all coming together; I cannot stop.

It's around this time that a voice in my head says, *"Dano, go inside and write your book."* It has whispered this line frequently over the last year, and on some days it talks quite loudly. Today for some reason, it starts shouting, like the thunder coming into focus from distant rolls to immediate booms - confirming that heading inside is indeed a good idea. *"Dano, go inside and write your book."* Suddenly the words of the unwritten memoir begin spewing out of my mind right before me: the keyboard would be like a big bowl I throw under them to try to catch and preserve as many as possible. The lines seem to write themselves, like my internal monologue got knocked up by wide-eyed observation; sentences gestate in my mind until one day they need to be born onto the page, and it's my obligation to nurture them into the composition that they have the potential to be. I think they're pretty good, too, and I think the voice's suggestion is a good one.

Only there's another layer, deeper inside. One that I can hardly identify because it's not a voice or plan or mission: it *is* me. It's Dad's voice advising me at eight years old, as I second-guess the completion of my first lawn-mowing job, to "never start a job you can't finish." It's the duty of completing the project, not so much to get tree limbs to the curb before the city truck comes around on Wednesday, but because finishing the job is just *what you do*. The neighbor didn't ask me to take care of her yard, it was only natural for me to volunteer my help. I was wound up and in my zone, and writing had to wait until lightening and darkness forced me indoors.

***

When I thought about the topics I'd focus on in writing a book, they seemed to boil down to fundamental truths like living in the present, helping others as part of a community, and visualizing goals intently until they become reality. So it seems contrary to spend time resting on my laurels, writing about the experiences. I mean, what kind of forward progress am I making sitting writing about the past? It's looking backwards, at what was, not training for what is coming next. Or so it appeared.

December. All my tri gear made it into the basement, neatly piled on a metal rack. Well, there was also a pile of towels and my wetsuit in a bag, and a big clear bin of other miscellaneous equipment and stuff from the garage that I didn't want subjected to the Wisconsin winter temperatures. My bike is stationary on its trainer, next to a stalled in-progress stack of suggested workout papers. The sacred off-season offers time to collect everything that comprised racing all summer. What needs cleaning, repaired, replaced? What should I sell, give away, or just trash? And, of course the million-dollar question "what new gear do I want?" Perhaps a little laurel-resting is indeed in order.

I have an overflowing manila folder on my desk labeled "Ironman," where I collected little things from all over the house, slowly removing them from daily display and cherishing them in an archive. Some day, these might become pages in a scrapbook about the big day, maybe pages about the whole year of training. They will encourage and direct me as I write down this memoir. I appreciate a scrapbook's ability to contain authentic but not-quite-flat things like a race wristband or original number bib; I appreciate the printed word's ability to summarize ephemeral emotional ups and downs felt over the course of years.

As computers overflow with gigabytes of unedited digital snapshots, the classic "printed photographs" or "albums" I grew up with grow scarcer. I feel that although even more memories are being preserved, they are seldom curated - and as such, abundant but lacking direction; saved, but not accessible for posterity. I somehow doubt that my progeny will discover a dusty spindle of CD-ROM's in a box in my house, place them into a machine that can still read them, and be so moved by the images themselves that captions aren't necessary. Something makes me want to round up the remnants of good times and prepare them for sharing. In the same vein, the printed word on the page offers a permanence to one fleeting day - one fleeting year... four fleeting years - in this racing life. Here we are.

If I don't rest on my proverbial laurels and focus on putting it together now, when will I? More new data will always keep pouring in as long as I keep living a life in which I'm making things happen worth filling a book. It's hard for a task-oriented person who feels the need to constantly stay on top of day-to-day needs to step aside and dig into what appears to be a non-critical-path project. But unless I intentionally take the time, I'll always be rushing on to the next project, and never really celebrate the significance of what I've just accomplished, or realize what I've learned from it. It's a debriefing, an historical preservation, a victory party.

When will I have the time to write, among my training and my regular job and my other interests? If you want to make something a priority, you have to let the other things calling your name just wait a bit. Better yet, learn what times of day you have energy that lends itself best to creativity, productivity, physicality, contemplation, or rest - and capitalize on them. How do I carve out the time for reflection, let alone making progress on a memoir? Well, Dano, how did you carve out time to train for those big races?

Where should I start? Just like the training plan: figure out what I want to do, identify and remove whatever could prevent me from getting there, and begin taking the steps to do the work, gain confidence, and complete it. Won't devoting my time to writing prohibit me from spending time doing other things that might help people? Perhaps so - but perhaps the product of the writing itself could turn out to make some kind of difference.

From the time I began training for that first big triathlon, I also made my first venture into the blogosphere. It seemed like all the cool kids were doing it. I chronicled the season with pretty good diligence. It was a good forum for sharing photos, recapping races, recounting anything particularly adventurous, and eventually musing curiously at the very patterns or concepts that drive me. "Share" with whom, I'm not entirely sure: as with many blogs today, the total readership may have been quite modest, but the benefit of what has often been prescribed as "journaling" likely inspired me into quiet moments of self-reflection, and reflection on the beautiful and robust experiences of life, through the lens of endurance training. I was not only pursuing my goals, I was also a spectator.

Fortunately, when I eventually sat down in front of a blank screen, trying to muster the confidence and methodology for writing down the "memoir" that my inner voice told me to write, I realized that I had already made a lot of progress. One of my first steps was reading over all the text from my blogs, and putting some of that text together to get this piece moving. I hadn't realized that by simply making small periods of time to consider and document the things I noticed, I would end up with some 30,000 words filling 83 pages in aggregate. Why be afraid of starting a project that the numbers say I'm quite capable of? The stigma of the blank screen was debunked.

My desire to grow this 'book' idea into a reality grew, and I began to make myself more accountable by telling some of my closer friends that I was working on it. One evening at dinner with a fellow tri-friend, airing out some of my ideas, the title struck me, and suddenly all the things I was thinking of trying to say were heading in one particularly distinct direction. Since that night - years ago now - getting down to business on the memoir somehow seemed more urgent. Each month that passed made me feel almost unbearably lethargic, though I tried to remind myself of the importance of my daily balance. I watched for chunks of time to put my head down, get wound up, and ride it on in to completion.

When I do, will anyone pick it up and read it? I don't know. If my words can resonate with someone else in a way that helps them see the world a little more fully, re-examine some part of their life more compassionately, or achieve a goal more successfully, I'd be glad that what once felt like intentional laurel-resting was in fact achieving "progress."

There's a lot more to "training" than trying to develop better muscles, and there's a lot more to "racing" than trying to be the first one across the line. I know it's different for everyone, but here are a few things that I've noticed.

PART I
A REALLY BIG RACE

THE BIG ONE

"And *then*, you run a marathon." The marathon alone is one of the most beautiful and challenging feats a human can undertake; when placed after 2.4 miles of swimming and 112 miles of bicycling, it's elevated to another plane. When something as big as a marathon becomes one item on a list, that must be one heck of a list.

From the moment I decided to sign up for Ironman, I wanted it to be big. I wanted to take on something impressive and overcome it. I wanted to do something much harder than ordinary people do in the course of their ordinary lives, even though that's exactly what I considered myself. When setting out on a long journey, we can't know in advance whether it will be transformative, but we can sense its magnitude, and we can choose how we approach it. It may not appear that we can choose how profoundly an experience will impact us, but when we choose to commit deeply, we are changed systemically.

Beginning the day I signed up, and persisting throughout the season, I made choices that kept the race big. Curiously, my first nod to the size of the race was writing a plan and starting small, respecting that the end-goal was much too challenging for the person leaving the sign-up table, but cultivating faith that the year ahead would be long and my preparation would be diligent.

I decided to blog the journey, for the initial intentions of catharsis, accountability, and fundraising potential. Regularly writing caused me to remain alert for events and realizations worth noting; the practice of shaping words into concise blog entries helped me identify what some of it meant, that might otherwise have gone unnoticed. (OK, sometimes they weren't particularly *concise*, but the process of digesting was set in motion). I tried to keep my mind open to experiences, from discovering new places and meeting new people, to finding more beauty in things that appeared simple, to finding comfort in routine and experience.

Because I committed to my goal from the beginning, I believed in myself in a way that I hadn't been accustomed to; my frame of reference for the whole season was set on an upward trajectory that just would not accept defeat. Bumps and changes, yes - but not defeat. I frequently reviewed my goals and plans, and adapted them as life's forces nudged me in various directions. I accepted that pain would naturally occur alongside joy, and suddenly pain lost a layer of its sting. Setbacks were guaranteed to occur within this one specific, manageable goal, so I approached them with simple re-evaluation, not weighty wallowing or overgeneralized self-judgment.

The framework of my life situation leant itself well to this kind of training pursuit. The sport was part of the culture in my city, and after sign-up day I became privy to a flurry of open-ended invitations beckoning "hey, we should train together!" I had a team of charity athletes whose encouragement and mission would help me stick with it. With discipline, I had enough expendable income to buy the gear I thought would make the biggest impact, but the humility to stay pragmatic about the gadgetry in favor of strength - of body, mind, and character. I had a job that gave me a good outlet for producing good-quality work at a level commensurate with my skill set, but also gave me a large amount of flexibility and time off that would lend itself well to training. The more I looked for ways the framework of my life was conducive to this large undertaking, the more grateful I felt.

I had my health and wanted to celebrate it. Sometimes I read stories in the magazines and books of the sport, of athletes who have overcome intense adversity to train, or to even move at all. Athletes with missing limbs, lost eyesight, or resources depleted by war have rewritten unthinkable misfortune into resilience and have somehow overcome them to reach even the starting line. These athletes are a picture of human accomplishment; what am I? Aren't I just a guy who's going after a personal dream? In comparison, I could have let my dream be very small, but this would do nothing but diminish my own opportunity to experience life more fully.

As the year of training went by... as the race went by... as the years went by after the race, ideas brewed inside me that went beyond swimming, biking, and running. I wrote down what I discovered: ideas about the qualities of life that I'd like to cultivate, and would love to see cultivated by other people. Maybe some would dismiss these ideas as overly-idealized hyperbolae, but just as I had allowed my race to be big, so too were the things I understood it to stand for.

I feel comfortable telling a 'normal' guy's story, because race-born truths are relevant not just to triathletes, but also to those who have never attempted a triathlon. Maybe some are universal. Ideas from a common age-grouper like me might just spark interest in anyone, and have the potential to make the world a little better off.

SIGNING UP

Triathlon is a sport made up of several; it's one race composed of swimming, biking, and running in succession, timed from start to finish, including the transitions from one to the next. In a way, it's simple: swim, bike, run. But in its collection of three sports, triathlon takes on a personality of its own. Practicing all three sports can have profound impacts on the body, since it recruits nearly every muscle; making triathlon a worthwhile component of a healthy life challenges you to understand yourself.

Its most basic requirements are simply pants, a bike, and a helmet - though it's easy to spend almost endless money on equipment. As such, amateurs can enjoy the success of completing an event while seasoned professionals can struggle to find the perfect balance of output to win one. You don't really have to be particularly "good" at swimming, biking, or running or walking to make it through a triathlon. At most local races, the field includes those competing for top positions, and those completing the race for their own accomplishment. The sport is designed to accommodate the entire spectrum between.

The collection of swim-bike-run, "triathlon," takes several sizes, from sprint (usually a 1/4-mile swim, a 10-mile bike ride, and a 3.1-mile run), to International (a 1500-meter swim, a 40-kilometer bike ride, and a 10-k run), to half-iron, to full iron-distance (a 2.4-mile swim, a 112-mile bike ride, and then a 26.2-mile marathon run). While none of these is a piece of cake, and while each certainly require intense preparation to *win*, perhaps the most fabled, celebrated, iconic distance is the long iron-distance.

When Ironman made its annual visit to Wisconsin in 2008, I had been a runner for 13 months, and had finished two local sprint triathlons. Just watching the big race, I felt intensely enthusiastic - a feeling of gratification just being close to the individuals taking it on. That September evening, I volunteered as a course marshal, helping direct age-group athletes as they made their way through the run course, under ever-darkening skies and the arrival of an ominous thunderstorm. I lingered under the relative cover of a building's overhang and broke the night silence with my individual cheers as they came into the building's light, shuffled past, and disappeared again onto the dark bike path beside the lake. Out of sight, miles in the distance, lights shined and music blared as the announcer shouted the finishers' names until the race ended at midnight.

The following morning, registration opened for the next year's race. It was the kind of decision my heart made, insisting that if I just had the courage to sign up - to dive in - that I would have the wherewithal to ultimately put everything else together.

Over the years, it had pulled at my heart strings. I kept thinking: "I want to do this." One year it was impressive, the next year it was impressive and really motivating, the next year I stood alongside the course, volunteering in the dark. I had a dollop of experience in the sport, and it was impressive and motivating ... and somehow doable. Not because I felt fit enough to complete it the day I signed up, but because I knew I had the strength to commit to becoming ready over the course of a year.

A line formed early in the morning and stretched out of sight around the race-site parking lot. The same place was packed with rows and rows of brilliant bikes just the day before, now transformed strangely back into its work-a-day form, waiting for morning commuters to begrudgingly fill up the stalls with their cars. A door separated the long wait in line outside from the actualization of signing up inside: the same door that athletes run through on race day, after finishing the long bike ride, on their way to beginning the marathon.

Through this door was something very challenging, and quite unknown. A transition. It was the same portal that I would enter one year later, about to try something I had never done - running a marathon after swimming 2.4 miles and biking 112 miles. When I signed up, I had never done any one of these.

My morning sign-up journey began not far from this door. Not knowing what to expect, I arrived super-early and was one of the first people in line. If something is important and you want to be sure you get it, you go early. If you don't want to worry about traffic, make excuses about construction or parking, or whine about being in the back of a long line, take control, think ahead, and go early. This much I knew going into it. Perhaps I went a little overboard arriving at 4:30 a.m., but this was my first nod to the race's larger-than-life scale.

I can recall high school summers staying up so late that my dad got up for work before I went to bed. But once I became a "grown up" and realized the advantages of getting up early, it's become my way of life. I felt right at home sitting in a line alongside others with the ambition to get out of bed for the purpose of going after what they want, front-loading their days with accomplishments. I felt energized being close to people so hard-working and motivated that they would add this pursuit on top of all the rest of their life priorities.

Though it was very early, people were cheerful, optimistic, and friendly. One guy had a big box of coffee that he offered around to anyone interested. People chatted quietly and passed the hours getting to know each other, almost always starting with "have you done this before?" and moving on to topics like other favorite races, plans for the next season, hopes and dreams… and occasionally - but seldom significantly - their day jobs.

Pretty much anyone can sign up for the race - all you have to do is show up, get in line, and pay the fee. At one point in the line-waiting process, I got up to use the bathroom, and struck up a conversation with a young lady also signing up for her first time - she marveled "we are *paying* to do this to ourselves?!" I'm sure the fee is prohibitively expensive for some, so it might be venturing slightly into elitism to call the race *completely* open to everyone, but no qualifications or tests are necessary to get in. Almost none of the characteristics by which people judge one another restrict entry here. In many ways, the race is democratic and egalitarian.

Anyone willing to dare to take it on is welcome to the registration table. One single starting line stretches before all of them. Young, old, fat, thin, amateur, veteran - it's ours for the taking. To sign up, you don't even have to believe in yourself or feel courageous, I suppose, but it's likely that the year ahead will change you, if you let it. Even I, a regular guy who had never competed in college sports, who would not use the label "athlete" on himself, who had simply tried a couple local triathlons and completely loved them, was welcome here.

I left that place grinning ear to ear, with a piece of paper confirming the commitment I had just jumped into. The race wasn't a year away - only the finish line was. Where to begin?

HOW TO WORRY

Through much of my life, I've been pretty much an expert on worrying. I have years of experience worrying about big things, little things, irrational things, completely fictitious situations, and more. In racing, there are plenty of things to worry about, regardless of whether the race is short or long, big or small, important or inconsequential. But this new pursuit presented a fresh environment for rebuilding myself, and although it appeared compartmentalized at first, the things I learned in fact had profound impacts on the habits I carry through all my life.

Some worries have to do with deep-rooted fears that are hard-wired into human beings for the benefit of their species' survival: *what if I get seasick in the water, what if I panic, what if I drown?* Other worries are popular in racing but not quite so drastic: *what if I flat on the bike, or it breaks down, or I crash; what if my legs cramp on the run, or one of my injuries of past years comes back?* Alongside a long list of equipment is a parallel list of things that can go wrong with each piece, including forgetting to bring it altogether. It's no wonder some people stress about racing.

Sometimes I hear even more poignant questions: *what if I'm not strong enough, what if I don't make it? What if I fail?* When I hear these rhetorical questions spoken out loud, I wonder how many people vocalize them just to fish out a response, from others or themselves. Maybe because they're just not sure. They're not sure they believe in what they have done to prepare, or they're not willing to be committed deeply. I wonder whether these types of questions are spoken in hopes that they will be met with a reassuring word from someone else - but belief in oneself can only honestly come from within. Pragmatically, what would be the use in worrying about whether I'm strong enough? Race day gives a definitive answer.

Curiously, racing for me has been a welcome reprieve from worry, a microcosm instead filled with exhilaration and joy. In spite of all the things that can go wrong, every single time, and in spite of my habit of worrying. I think because I had to start from scratch, I was able to commit to a new paradigm, leaving the unnecessary baggage - that thrived in other parts of my life - at the doorstep of each training session. Maybe I recognized that ultimately, this pursuit was just a hobby, and even pretty serious failures within it wouldn't ruin me overall. Fortunately, learning to take risks, shed worries, and succeed in new ways turned out to have everything to do with the rest of my life.

I suspect that beginning my endurance journey as a charity athlete with Team In Training made a big difference, too. The whole tone of coaching and mentoring I received was positive and empowering, without focus on competition, but instead on mission, inner strength, and ultimately going the distance. "Being strong" and "going the distance" were immediately metaphorically-charged for me, and from the beginning I associated distance racing with the manifestation of my own ideals. Racing was meant for fun, for joy - it's a hobby, and why should a hobby be something that generates stress? If it does, what about it could be modified?

As my year of training began, with 364 days to go and a lot of preparation ahead, I thought about all the things I might worry about - all those crazy triathlon things that might go wrong - and began compiling them into a long list. *Swim panic, flat tire, forgotten shorts.* I even thought about things that I heard other people worrying about, even though I wasn't worried about them myself. *Drowning, mental breakdown, projectile vomiting.* To be thorough, I broadened the list to include all those concerns in the rest of my life I had been mulling over. *Jobs, relationships, vacations.* To be sure I thought of everything, I broke the big race down by time of day, by sport, by location. *Broken goggles, stolen bike, pooping in shorts.*

I came up with a long list of eligible worries or concerns, ranging from things that could go wrong with my equipment, to pieces of equipment that I didn't own, to doubts about my own athletic ability, to the weather. In each case, I kept trying to lengthen the list and add more specifics, trying to group the issues in a logical way, and arrange them according to their relative severity. I noted the ones that were truly relevant to me - contrasted with the ones that seemed irrelevant or trivial. It became evident that some anxieties stemmed from other, deeper fears; I could go after the beast's heart. A part of this list might be called my "weaknesses."

But of course it was not all worry - through this exercise, I had a lot of positive thoughts, too. A few races under my belt and the amount I enjoyed them laid great groundwork, albeit modest. Moderation, patience, and perseverance came to mind as attributes that could be particularly useful in the long season and long miles ahead. I could have compared myself to others, particularly those who were fitter, taller, or more athletically-experienced than me, but knew that these comparisons wouldn't get *me* to the finish line any faster. Instead, my own individual experiences like engineering problem-solving and yoga-breathing were on my side. The list helped me see my starting place, and be honest with myself. What had I done so far with success, I asked, and where did I want to end up? So there I was, with a comprehensive list of my weaknesses and worries, right beside my strengths and goals, and I put them together...

Voila, a training plan!

An effective training plan boils down to the systematic transformation of fears, worries, and weaknesses into the dramatic probability of success - however you define success. It builds on what one believes in and is best at doing. It defines the level of specific performance desired, while managing the problems that threaten to interfere. It lays out a personal path toward a personal goal, which may overlap with others' paths, but is not the same path - and as such avoids one person being stuck behind another. In these ways, a triathlon training plan is fundamentally similar to a plan for improving any kind of situation.

Every training plan is individual, and none is perfect, but I know why my plan worked for me. It started big, with goals and concepts, laid out over the course of my training period - one year. I'll share my goal, it was no secret: "finish Ironman Wisconsin 2009 and have a good time." The concepts to get there came from my lists of worries and weaknesses, carefully prioritized from what I thought was actually a big deal and what was just an overactive mind. For me, these concepts on the way to my goal included *"get comfortable in the water," "have a great time biking all summer while training to be able to bike for a long time"* and *"take care of the injuries that have been barriers to being the best runner I can be this year."* Other life goals aren't insignificant to the mix: work full-time, volunteer, care for my home, gardens, and pets. For me, training had to remain positive, balanced and exemplary of a well-rounded, healthy lifestyle. Looking back, had I not approached training in this way, I think it could easily have consumed much of my life, rather than enhance it. Note that I have not yet mentioned a single mile, minute or muscle.

Once the goals were clear, and the concepts of the training - the biggest objectives - were defined, I could make decisions accordingly. I spent time finding and reading the most reputable books on racing long, on swimming efficiently, and on the motivating stories of those who had done it. I sought out conversations with others who had been through it. But as I read and listened, I tried to pay attention to my own goals, and silently think about which of these thousands of pages of advice would work best for me. A lot of people are dying to share their stellar, "best-selling" advice that might be completely irrelevant to my own goals. In this race, and in all the preparation for it, I was ultimately accountable to no one but myself, because my goals are no one else's but my own.

I looked to the science of periodization as an overarching concept - slowly building up hours of training over several weeks, then backing down, then building back up a little more, and so on in a calculated, scientific way - but tailored to my life schedule. Training is supposed to enhance life through health and balance, not replace its finest unique opportunities. By the time I signed up for my big race, I already had some vacations planned, which were perfect times to focus on my personal life and break from training. When I crafted my training plan, I placed the big build-ups before my breaks, and then headed out of town knowing that I had accomplished what I needed, and deserved the quality rest. I never had a reason to regret the days off because I had taken care of the hard work - and I was able to more fully enjoy both of these because their purposes were more clear. Commitment to days off turned out to be just as - if not more - important than days on.

As I set about preparing my body and mind for the task ahead of me, I also had a year to work on that long list of gear-related worries. Addressing this list was hardly "work" - it was a lot of fun, because it involved a favorite pastime of triathletes: buying gear! Actually, I am not made of money, and I tried to keep at bay all the ads and friends' assertions promising a faster, happier finish from their piece of equipment, because in my heart I knew that spending a lot of money wasn't necessary to achieving my true goals. It wasn't even actually necessary for going faster - *there's no substitute for the engine*. I just needed the right equipment to meet my goals, at an appropriate level of risk.

I bought good-quality equipment that had a reputation for reliability, and took good care of it. I took the time to learn how to change a tire, then I practiced, then I practiced again with faster compressed-CO_2 canisters. To manage concerns like "broken goggles," I simply kept an older spare pair in my race bag. I pondered seemingly eternal debates like "are tubular tires or clinchers better?" and decided that the more versatile, interchangeable, repairable (and less expensive) clincher was the best match for my racing credo. I bought ridiculous-looking alien-mask-style goggles after determining that these offered great visibility, comfort, and protection if bumped. I opted out of a lot of fun technical gadgetry to keep myself from getting too bogged down in the details; I wanted to learn to understand my body in the simple terms of "easy" and "hard."

I looked at a lot of bikes before buying an end-of-model-year Quintana Roo, the tried-and-true original developer of the triathlon-specific frame geometry, and still a well-respected leader in the tri-bike world. I was willing to spend some bucks to get a light and stiff carbon-fiber frame, with high-quality components that would last me a long time with good reliability. I test-rode some even-more-expensive bikes, but (fortunately) this one just seemed to fit me just right. I knew I would do my part to care for and maintain this beautiful machine for many miles - far beyond one race. It could stay right in bed with me. And, frankly, I felt that I deserved it. I had spent the last two years riding a second-hand road bike that wasn't even my size. The time had arrived to begin a new era in riding; the time had arrived for me to make an investment in my commitment to myself.

A year is a big chunk of time - enough time to accomplish a lot. It had better be, because we don't get all that many of them to live (77.9 in the United States in 2010, according to the CDC.) For some goals, I level with myself and say a year simply isn't enough time. For example, if I wanted to qualify for the Boston Marathon, I would have to run so much faster that if I tried to do it too soon, I'm confident I would injure myself and be set back badly. Cue *"take care of the injuries that are barriers to the best runner I can be this year."* Knowing that I had a whole year, and a good plan, I was able to ramp up gradually and healthily for the big tri. My results in other events gave me confidence that a year was the right amount of time to ramp up to my ultimate goal: finish the Ironman.

One of the very best ways to gain experience with racing is just that: to race! As I set out on my training journey, certain races were milestones in my preparation, each for different reasons. The journey began mostly on faith, but was soon supplemented with good planning, then practice which yielded experience. Experience was a powerful mechanism for striking off the list those worries that turned out to be bogus, while highlighting others that were still problematic. Things went wrong and things went right in each race, and I archived the experiences of how to deal with them and move on - or at least ideas for how to manage them for the next time. Often, things that went wrong made for great stories, but had very little actual consequence otherwise, demonstrating that worrying doesn't do much good anyway. I had plenty of faith to get started, and kept plenty of it through the season, and supplemented it with dabs of proof along the way.

A YEAR OF TRAINING

I had a year to prepare. A year is a long time - long enough for the lakes to freeze close, then reopen again, then steam in the cool mornings as fall returns again. My year of training included my first marathon... and my second. It was energized by group training, and solidified with long solo sessions. Without really doing anything more than practicing the sport, I began making the gradual shift from novice to somewhat-experienced; I slimmed and strengthened far beyond the general population's average. I made a point to stop and think often about high and low days, which turned into a habit: the ubiquitous high and low tidbits in every otherwise ordinary day became more visible. Paying attention throughout the year kept the year from flying by unnoticed - and made the year that much more significant.

I might have been inclined to latch on to the insurmountably long distance I was going to attempt, and immediately run out the door to "train" in whatever way I could think of. Just go as hard and as long as I could. Crank my alarm clock back to 4:00 a.m., put on a sweat suit, drink a bunch of raw eggs, and run up the Capitol stairs. Less epic though it may have been, I started from a seated position, on a sunny afternoon at a picnic table in the park where I did my first triathlon. With a pad of paper and a couple books, I wrote down my limiters and strengths, and assigned purpose to each month and week.

Without having tried it before, I knew that a year was long enough to burn out - even pursuing something very important to me - if I didn't allow it to live harmoniously with other things I liked in life. I believe in the tortoise and the hare, starting slowly and building up. I believe in the power of a plan and overarching goals written strongly enough that they do, in fact, include room for adapting to changing conditions - and enjoying a life that embraces those goals without shoving everything else good to the wayside.

It was a good move, because I signed up in mid-September. Had I immediately begun a regimen of long bike rides or lake swims, I would have soon been disappointed with the onset of fall. As the leaves changed from green to vivid yellow, orange, and red, and the snow began to fall, my training went largely inside and began with a focus on fundamentals. I was preparing to go long, but I knew that if I started short instead, backing off the distance in favor of improving my technique, I'd develop the technical aptitude to go long as a result of efficiency, rather than just brute force.

I was fortunate that the college right down the street from my office offered open lap swimming, and I made a habit of walking over at lunch time a couple times per week. Many people swim early in the morning, and I could have tried to be hard core and force myself to also do it that way. But I struggled with swimming - although I liked it in general, it tended to make me feel queasy, and I tended to have a sore stomach in the morning anyway. Conversely, I found that lunch-time swims broke up the day in the office, gave me more energy for the afternoon than a cup of coffee, and avoided my morning digestive distress altogether. I took advantage of the pool's proximity, adjusted my work schedule, and swam when I was able to feel good about it rather than loathe it. Consistent with my training goal itself, it was about efficiency. The setting for the workout complemented the goal of the workout: get comfortable in the water.

In the pool, rather than jumping in and swimming up and down the blue line as many times as I could, I poked up and down the lane practicing drills: catch-up, one-arm, no-arms, rolling, fingertip-drag, you name it. It wasn't about swimming a long way (yet), it was about teaching my muscles how I wanted them to operate; it was about efficiency. My top goal was to become comfortable in the water, so I tried to frame the drills in a playful way - developing balance as the water supported me, I was a capable sea creature moving and turning. I worked my way from splashy to smooth, and by spring had become more confident that I could swim the distance, safely under the cut-off.

Snow didn't put a damper on my training. I'm constantly pulled to being outside, regardless of racing goals - though I did find that shoveling snow was a great way to get my heart rate up. I was more inclined to shovel for the neighbors as well, to intentionally expend more effort. (Medically-inclined friends later noted that this can also be a great way to damage your back, so use caution). Sledding combined fearless rushes with tough climbs. In the bleak midwinter, the yoga studio was respite from the cold. In the winter season when I focused on the fundamentals of my body, yoga was one of the best ways to get in touch with myself and the ways I was capable of moving.

I give a lot of credit to the people in Madison who bike year-round, in spite of the weather. Admittedly, I wasn't one of them. So to retain the basics of my cycling ability, I connected my bike to a trainer in my basement, where I could keep my legs reminded of that circular motion, and my rump reminded of that little saddle. Christmastime brought a new beginning to my trainer-time: Santa brought a 6-DVD set of the Tour de France, which turned out to be an exciting motivator. As I watched the race surge toward a stage's finish, I'd find myself upshifting and sweating to keep up.

Even better, as a gift, my brother loaned me a special set of cranks in support of my year-long training goal. A bicycle's cranks transfer power from the pedals into the chain. Usually the two pedals are fixed in position opposite one another, so as one gets pushed down by one foot, the other comes up. These particularly masochistic devices have clutches inside that make each side move independently. They force the legs to work independently, teaching the muscles to make perfect circles with each revolution, so no energy is wasted by one pedal working *against* the other, even for a fraction of each revolution. Because tiny fractions really add up over 112 miles. After my friends at the bike shop installed the cranks, I excitedly connected my bike to the trainer and jumped on. Five minutes later, I was too exhausted to continue.

On March 5th, the temperature made it up into the mid-50's, and I had no choice but to take my bicycle for our first outdoor ride of the season. I took my road bike because I didn't want to get my racing bike dirty - only to inevitably bring it back inside to the trainer anyway. Plus I was too chicken to use the special cranks out on the road. The decision turned out to be wise since the bike path was a mess of grit and melt-water - but the kind of mess that indicates the welcome rebirth of spring. Every little thing about the ride felt fresh and exciting: blowing up the tires, checking over the bike's safety, getting my gear out of its winter box, even feeling a little wobbly from not being locked in to the trainer. When I got out onto the path, I could feel the results of my wintertime strength-training, and felt even a little giddy saying "on your left" for the first time in four months.

My running finally developed a regular routine, and though many days it was still hard to get out the door, I often found it enjoyable once I got started, even through the winter. For the first time in my life, I put 300 miles on a pair of shoes. As I retired that pair of Mizuno's, I thanked them for being a trusted companion in sun, rain, snow, and sleet; from 14 below to 78 above; from training to racing; from Wisconsin to Ohio to Florida to Texas to Nebraska; and indeed in sickness and in health.

I found myself posing them in front of the fireplace for a

photo before donating them, considering what "retirement" might really mean. I grapple with the balance between preparing for something to come, and living in the thing that is now. Anticipation of the next thing to come helps make its eventual arrival that much sweeter - but how fun would a triathlon be if I focused so much on getting into my running shoes that I forgot to sit back and enjoy the bike ride?

As the spring races arrived, I did a combination of racing and supporting. At a local 5k, I gathered up friends and worked at the water station. After running in several races, it was a good experience to be the guy handing out the water for a change - it felt fair and good. The next month - April - I raced hard at a favorite local 8k drawing some 20,000 people, nearly 1/10 the population of Madison itself. I ran hard in spite of the stormy winds and torrential downpour, which turned out to be some of my very favorite weather for running. My new PR earned me a spot in one of the next year's top starting corrals.

I entered a new chapter in my running career, a training schedule where "secondary" races were chosen and prioritized based on what they meant for me personally and physically. I had signed up for both the Green Bay and Madison marathons, on back-to-back weekends. The plan was to run Green Bay, then in Madison either switch to the half, run very slowly, or just skip it altogether. Well, I halfheartedly got in the car to drive 2 hours to Green Bay, alone. Just as I arrived, I realized that I had forgotten my wallet. I went to the expo, where they gave me my packet nonetheless, but when I looked around didn't see anyone I knew. I couldn't pay for a hotel. I couldn't buy dinner; I couldn't buy a stinking gel or bar. Fortunately, I did have just over a half-tank of gas, and a couple hours later I arrived back in Madison with my first crisp, uncirculated race number. The following weekend, I pulled myself back together and PR'd by 30 minutes in my second full-marathon, practically in my own back yard.

Spring and Memorial Day gave way to summer, and the meat of my training schedule. I was happy with the way my season was coming together, with a nice organic flow. At the dawn of summertime, with six months to go, I recognized that a new phase of training had arrived: the long part. To succeed in my big race, I'd have to show up healthy and ready for my long sessions, and maintain consistency in between. So although I had excelled at writing down goals and charting a brilliant training schedule, I still had to complete one critically important step: get to work. The race requires physical preparation: beyond nebulous feelings, the proverbial rubber did eventually have to hit the literal road. Neither goals nor training can succeed without the other. I had to put down my pen, scribing my theses on the philosophical meaning of racing - and go train.

While my muscles became stronger, gaining experience helped me go faster as a result of simply getting smarter. I've never considered myself a big powerhouse, but I do feel intelligent. I paid attention to what went right and wrong at each race, and where I found my energy. I learned how I fit into race morning: my risk tolerance for parking, my optimal time to get in the bathroom line, the best time to get in the bathroom line again, and the best place to stand among the field of athletes. I didn't try so much to be like other people, but instead watched what others did and decided which techniques fit me well and which I'd rather avoid.

I learned things only the races can teach: how to un-pin a gel from shorts while running, how to stop the bleeding where the pin stabbed me while un-pinning, how good a hat full of ice feels, how to persevere as the hours go by and stopping sounds more appealing. The night before the Green Lake triathlon, I had what I suspect is a common dream, of racing through the bike course and coming to an unmarked turn and going the wrong way. In the real race the next morning, as karma would have it I came out of transition and had to stop to figure out which way to go. I learned to not only arrive early, but take a few minutes to check over the course map, and walk the transitions. Perhaps most importantly, I learned to always look over my shoulder in the finishing chute to keep some sprinter from blocking my perfect photo, and to never be caught looking down at my watch as I crossed the finish line. I learned to try hard, and celebrate heartily.

Even as the training hours increased, I made a point to still live the life I wanted and not let the training consume me. I took time to rest so in general I didn't feel overly worn out, but when I stopped to think about it, I realized that all the training did, in fact, take up a lot of time. In August, my new race-wheels arrived, giving me an additional boost for my longest workouts - 300 and 330-minute bike rides. Sunday remained my most-prized "day off," serving as a control-alt-delete for all the rest of life as I washed clothes, tidied up, and prepared piles of food. Much of my blogging was relegated to the seated stillness of Sunday afternoon; my online status might as well have been "gone outside for the summer."

SMILING AT THE EDGE OF CONSCIOUSNESS

Even before I discovered running or endurance sports, I discovered what has turned out to be their inseparable companion, which I would be remiss not to mention. I remember entering my first hot yoga class timidly, but boldly trying everything the instructor said. I had no idea what was next, and therefore had no sense of how I might restrain my effort. I had no reason to hold back from anything, and in spite of being completely novice, had a breakthrough class to remember: I had a beginner's mind. I had nothing to compare it to, nothing to judge. I left the class physically drained to the point my body felt weak and indeed very strange all over. I felt mentally strange as well, knowing that I had just nudged a new world of being at the edge - if even just for 90 minutes. If even for just a minute at a time.

The styles of yoga to which I have been drawn are the more intense varieties - vinyasa flow, constantly moving for an hour, and hot yoga, made up of challenging static poses in a regimented sequence. The purpose of the hot room is threefold: encourage the muscles to become more limber, encourage sweating as a body-housekeeping mechanism, and develop peace of mind in spite of the physical conditions. Plus, it feels great when the winter relentlessly deals temperatures below zero. I particularly like how yoga is organic. The body can be intensely strengthened under only its own weight and stretched under its own strength - without the purchase of any fancy equipment, but instead with one's own intentions. In the same moment that the body stretches and flexes against its own movement, the mind tries to call out concerns and change the body's course; this practice is the chance to reign in the mind's chatter when it explodes on some tangent of its own.

I've attended hundreds of classes, which have been not just fundamental to my strength and range of motion for the benefit of athletic pursuits, but essential to developing a sense of resolve and determination in spite of challenging conditions. In class, I aim to simply breathe, move, and explore. I don't have to say anything, and the instructor's cues tell me what to do next so I don't even have to think. In the heat, through the movement both on my own and as part of the moving-group, I often feel inner peace and joy because I am able to recognize and truly believe that there is nothing to fear in the moment, even if something feels uncomfortable. I have developed a craving for the sensations that come with moments of intensity: limbs like jelly, heart pounding, even feeling about to pass out. I've come to love this healthy self-induced discomfort, feeling safe to explore my edge with curiosity inside the studio, and learning that I can survive challenging situations outside of it. I discovered a lot about what it means to hang on... for just another second, which invariably gives way to another, then another.

In the studio where I practice, all abilities are welcome. The practice of yoga has nothing to do with one person's abilities compared to another's - or even with any one person's particular abilities - but everything to do with a personal intention and a vision inward. One person may approach it as a spiritual journey while the person right beside may want to simply get stronger. I enjoy being in a place without right or wrong, better or worse, but with only individual intentions.

Even though I don't have many conversations with fellow yogis as part of my practice, I feel a special sense of connection and energy simply by being in the same place, moving through the same class together.

It has been the perfect place to add strength training to my weekly regimen, improve my range of motion, and also practice calm. As I became an athlete, I increasingly enjoyed the intensity I could push myself into. Curiously, as a person I needed the practice of becoming calm and relaxed. As it turns out, the two have been congruous. ("Tri Therapy" - go figure.) The yoga practice focuses on deep, slow breathing, and gently acknowledging - then letting go of - the thoughts that come to mind. Not surprisingly, these are some of the same techniques suggested by therapists to calm anxiety in any situation: breathe, notice, release. In a lake with splashing and thrashing all around, a regular practice of the skills that can overcome the brain's natural panic responses will keep me swimming forward rather than stopping completely.

Yoga is my practice of mental discipline. Frequently, there comes a point in class when I want to stop and lay down, when my muscles scream that they don't want to do any more. But as the instructor speaks and the class begins to move, I somehow find my own movement originating from "I will try" instead of "I can't." Sometimes, I experience the inexplicable sensation of my body beginning to move in spite of my thinking it cannot. On some days, moving through the poses is almost an afterthought as I spend a whole hour trying to focus on my breath and letting go of the thoughts that keep trying to rush into my mind. *What will I have for dinner? How will I solve that problem? What is my next workout?* "Silence," I tell myself. I have deliberately set aside an hour, and gone to a specific physical place, to practice being nowhere but there for a period of time. In that commitment, I've opted out of other things, which will all simply have to wait. Phones and internets remain outside the studio.

No amount of thinking could do anything for me except take away from the very practice I went there to do.

Consequently, second-guessing this decision would result in not just missing the things that I decided not to do, but also missing the thing that I did decide *to* do. In a busy life, it's hard to pick one thing to do out of so many, but being unable to commit to one or another can end in simply doing *nothing* well. I've found great value in the practice of deliberately *mono-tasking*, focusing on the only true things that are real: one's self, and the exact instant in time one is living. This is a powerful place that can be extremely peaceful, even in the midst of challenging external circumstances. Some people focus on this place as a means of considering or accessing however they perceive God. I find that when I translate my focus on presence and inner peace from the yoga studio to the races, and on into other parts of my life, I find doors flinging open to reveal the joys that moved me deeply enough to write down this story for you.

There's something very intriguing and attractive about a challenging style of yoga that has to do with going to the edge. After only minutes inside a hot room, all sorts of changes happen. Sweat beads, then drips, and sometimes pours. My heart rate comes up, and in spite of practicing low, slow, deep breaths, my ability to feel smooth in breathing is challenged. As I move through various postures, my body begins to react with sensations that are not common in my day-to-day life. The sensation of letting go - sometimes of muscles relaxing that I did not know were hanging on. The sensation of blood rushing back into a joint after being bent for a long moment, feeling full and alive with each strong heart beat. As the practice intensifies - depending on the day - I experience a range of sensations and sometimes even flirt with feeling dazed and ready to collapse.

I'm not sure why I "like" these feelings, because they are uncommon and strange. They are, in one sense, uncomfortable, but in another extremely refreshing. During a deep backward bend, I feel primally vulnerable. Because I know I am safe in this place, I can explore it deeply, and feel absolutely fantastic. Euphoric. Sometimes being authentic to one's own goals means being vulnerable to the outside world - but the reward is great. It's easier to feel safe functioning within the larger, greater, more complicated world when grounded in faith in oneself.

As I get to know myself better on more levels, I'm able to push myself harder at races, at least when I want to. In the yoga studio, I can notice those times when I feel the mild anxiety that comes with certain discomforts, so that I can practice dealing with it and learning skills for when a larger problem presents itself: anywhere from a large open-water swim to a situation in which 'this had been an actual emergency.' The yoga studio has been my training grounds for the mental skills to deal with bad weather, motion sickness, panicky feelings, cramping, and unforeseen obstacles.

But like at the races, sometimes I wonder: why do some of the people around me look so miserable in their efforts, so laborious? If it's not fun, why pursue a hobby or sport? An hour into a 90-minute yoga class in a 100-degree room could be the perfect time to feel miserable. But the mental practice begs: right now, what can I do to lighten up? How can I continue to work in spite of fatigue? Indeed, although my body is uncomfortable, why should my emotional condition be unhappy?

For so many reasons, I find myself smiling through yoga classes - usually right from the beginning, then trying to call it back over and over again as the session intensifies. Although the effort is hard, I seek out the parts of myself that are stretching, realigning, detoxifying, replenishing - and I find them. As I look inward, the need to worry about anything else in life fades away, because in fact there's nothing to do about any of it in those moments. As I seek this phenomenon, often known as "presence," I can't help but feel: this is great! *I feel great!* My situation here in this place is wonderful! Like a wave, comfort rushes into me. It's only natural to smile.

Yoga gave me the kind of foundation I needed for all the rest to come into place the way it did. Making quite a leap of faith, buying a membership to the studio kept me accountable to my practice and was one of the first times in my life I made such a consistent dedication to either an athletic or a psychological pursuit - and ended up with literally life-changing results. My regular yoga practice has strengthened the core that holds my body upright in good form as hours of racing go by, and also the inner core that fortifies my values and holds up the goals that I request of myself.

A YEAR OF PRIORITIZING

With all its moving parts, triathlon might be considered the checklist-maker's dream sport. Checklist-making, along with thorough and relentless checking-off, has been one of my strengths as long as I can remember. Sometimes I've been criticized for being super-meticulous. I've been labeled "anal retentive" by friends familiar with my neat dwelling spaces, orderly files, and clean... well, everything. Hanging in balance with being overly rigid is the skill of prioritizing: determining what I really want and solving the puzzle of how to make it fit.

Let's be honest, There are worse compulsions than getting organized, if you must label me. I always thought it was a great way to be "ready" for any number of situations that might summon me to action. In triathlon, with all the different stuff to pack, bring to the race site, and place carefully in a tiny personal space at the transition rack, I was in my element. Things that came naturally to me were gaining me minutes on people grieving in the parking lot about how long it took them to do "x" because they forgot "y" or had a careless problem with "z." It's not that I needed to be in front of someone else or wanted them to fail, but I did feel vindicated that what I was once made fun of for did indeed get me somewhere: the finish line. Faster. I was changing - and so was the way I appreciated myself.

Training for a long race takes many, many hours - swimming, biking, running, sleeping; plus strength, flexibility, nutrition… planning, logging, charting, and more. I noticed my own lifestyle taking on new forms as the year unfolded: the "multisport lifestyle." Instead of feeling increasingly overwhelmed, I believe that with a hard look inward, the myriad of things that take up time in life can come into order with an honest evaluation. What's really important right now - and how can it fit into the mix? What's unimportant but still attracting my attention or taking my time, and how can I just let it go? What might have been relevant some other year, but not now? *Simplify*. Many of the things I wanted could all fit, as long as I added them in the right order, and allowed them to change shape a little bit from what I might have originally envisioned. *Be flexible*.

Truly, before any swimming, biking, or running began, sleeping came first: it was my foundation for health, clarity, and intensity to tackle each day. Being - or at least appearing - busy seems to be one of the most celebrated attributes of modern American life, and many people are quick to boast about how few hours they sleep each night. At the risk of being considered a lazy sloth by those who don't, I sleep eight hours a night, as regularly as possible. I suspect the reason why more people don't do it is that, simply put, it's hard. It's hard to say *no* to all kinds of things that sound worthwhile and fun, although too many hours of *yes* wears you down and leaves you with nothing but a bunch of *maybe*'s. The discipline of a good sleep schedule is harder than the effort of forcing oneself to stay awake, but the rewards are great.

An early morning swim down at the lake is one of the best ways to make friends, have energy all day, and appreciate nature's abundant peace through gently steaming glassy water and a brilliant orange sunrise. During summer's long days, getting up early is relatively easy and natural. But to have all this and sleep eight hours means going to bed around 9:00 p.m. - when the sun isn't even down. Other friends certainly aren't in bed. A lot of fun things are happening: shows are on TV, people have new photos and stuff to share online. Would I rather be awake putzing through the interwebs, or asleep rejuvenating for energy the next day to accomplish something worth writing about? I don't have a television. Actual real-life fun things happen all summer, too, like parties, campfires, dazzling rooftop events... The decision to dedicate time - quality time - to the personal, important things isn't something to complain about or make excuses for, it's something to celebrate. So I made choices each week, to go out, or intentionally skip certain opportunities in favor of high-quality training, and vice versa. Commitment requires decisions.

Backing up the clock, going to sleep at 9:00 p.m. also means winding down and preparing for sleep, and eating dinner before that, which ideally followed a workout by 30 minutes or less for optimal refueling. And so on through the day, I scheduled meals, rests, and activities to best fit together. For some, it's overwhelming and turns into a source of stress, but I tried to embrace the challenge as an optimization puzzle. This isn't to say that I never had to give things up, roll reluctantly with the bumps in daily life, or feel tension seeping in. It's not easy, and one of the hardest parts is that to optimize time, you have to plan ahead - which usually means committing to one thing over another. It's committing that seems to be one of the hardest things for people to achieve, because it means saying "no" ... in advance. It means letting an opportunity go by in favor of another one; prioritizing one goal over another. What the process taught me was to keep in mind what was really important, and seek guidance from that depth to make my decisions, stick with them, and feel good about them.

I discovered all sorts of ways to get more time out of a day. Good habits cascade - I keep a water bottle on my desk to stay well-hydrated, in turn get up frequently to use the bathroom and refill the bottle, in turn break up the long day seated at the computer screen... in turn take a route back to my desk that might even go outside for a moment of sunshine and fresh air, and maybe include a little stretching. My boss never gave me a hard time about any of it: he was excited about my training goal, and at the bottom line he was glad that I kept putting out results. Some might think that not working is a lousy way to get work done, but our bodies need physical movement and breaks from monotony. Our eyes need chances to look away from screens. So many people become wider, sicker, and sadder as they sit still hour after hour: this is not who I want to be.

When the computer ran a long process, I did pushups. I began sitting on a balance ball some of my day instead of my chair, opting to get a "free" core workout without taking a second more time. (I say "some" of the day because my sore abs taught me those things really work). My brilliant time-savers made me somewhat of a cultural anomaly at the Department of Transportation office, and I had to endure what felt like endless questions and remarks. At first, I thought these remarks were annoying because they weren't usually framed in a very positive way. I suspect that the negative tone, poking fun at me for being different, often gets added as someone tries to formulate something clever to say. I reframed it. I let the criticism roll away as irrelevant in terms of my goals, and when they expressed intrigue, I tried to use the opportunity to show my coworkers how easy it could be to make little changes toward a healthier lifestyle. Many people are afraid to share their personal endeavors, but I began to feel even better about myself because I believed that my goals were worthwhile and valid. Standing out a bit would be worth it if it meant a chance to inspire someone toward a healthier life.

The best way to create more time in my days was to systematically work as many of my goals as possible into my ordinary routines. Many of our routines develop arbitrarily, as a matter of course, and stay that way consistently with Newton's second law: until acted on by something else. Modifying a routine that might have developed arbitrarily to instead include something more productive can be tremendously powerful because of its consistency. If I replace an arbitrarily-grabbed beer with, say, tonic water, I might get most of the same desired result of sipping on something as I read, but take on fewer calories and feel fresher in the morning. With some research and only a little inspection, it became clear that I could make many improvements in my diet with easy substitutions: olive oil for vegetable oil, tea for soda, spices for buttery sauces, nuts for candy, and so on. Replacing one habit with a modified healthier version, over time and repetition, has compounding results.

The commute to work was nine miles each way, and since the route included crossing downtown on slower urban streets, I could travel the same distance on bike in about the same time as by car. In the afternoon traffic, I could actually get home faster by bike, thanks to the bike lanes on Washington Avenue. I'd have to give up listening to the radio, and I'd have to trade the ease of driving with the effort of riding - and carrying my lunch and change of clothes on my back - but would end up trading commute hours for training hours. *Found time.* Even one ride per week made a difference, I discovered as I started small. I didn't want to get discouraged by forcing myself to only go by bike and allow it to cause me inconvenience and suffering. Starting with a mix of car and bike allowed me to bring extra food and clothes on car-days, and carry less on bike-days. Like intense training days mixed with rest days, my bike-commuting effort was an approachable blend of hard and easy, and gave me particular satisfaction when I chose to bike - which inspired me to do it more.

As an aside, I think of bike commuting also as a kind of leadership. Cyclists are certainly still the underdogs on the road, but as this mode becomes more popular, my very presence as another body in the bike lane might just encourage someone else to try it, and help perpetuate the sport. Every time I make a legal stop, I'm one little case against "bikers never stop at red lights;" every time I arrive at the office on bike, I'm another day of proof that bike-commuting is in fact possible. I began noticing that my year of training might just radiate out positive energy beyond my own life goals, and beyond a single race day.

One day, a coworker approached me in an awkward way, starting a conversation with the kind of tone typical of rumor-milling or fear-mongering. In a secretive way, he quietly asked "hey Dan, I was thinking of maybe trying to get in a little better shape, do you think you could help me?" Of course, I was glad to offer some advice, and follow-up over time. The same people who seemed to ostracize me for my uncommon habits started to relate to me by asking "how's training going?" Indeed, I had to be willing to look different by sitting on my big green balance ball - but I began to also look different in my muscle tone, posture, and energy. I began to feel different about myself and feel more confident and more resilient. As I gained confidence born of something that I knew to be worthwhile, I was more comfortable in my own skin, in spite of being "different." I began to be asked questions about how to get in shape, how to eat better, how to get into running - and I was glad to answer them. I felt that being "different" might actually allow me to become a "role model."

In the last month of my training, my workouts came down to a few "breakthrough" race-simulation sessions, then a taper period for my body to recover and rejuvenate before the big race. Friends and coworkers had become interested in my journey over the course of the year, and often asked "how's training." As the taper period began in the last couple weeks before the race, it was time for me to respond, "done."

RACE REPORT:
IRONMAN WISCONSIN 2009

It was one of the most surreal experiences I've had. After a year of preparation and visualization, to actually take part in the day itself was more than reality. Surreal in the sense that it was real and more - bigger than reality. And for the same reasons, there was never any thought in my mind that I would not succeed.

The day began well before the 4:00 alarm went off. Ever since we ran the Disney World Marathon the previous January, Dad must have thought that 2:50 a.m. is a typical time to wake up for every big race. By 3:30, the smell of coffee had made its way under my door, into the bedroom where I was kind of still asleep. I got up and immediately began doing tasks, putting on the clothes neatly laid out the night before, packing my gear. I had delivered my bike and transition bags the day before, and I wasn't worried that everything I needed was contained in them.

When we arrived on site around 5:20 a.m., the sky was already starting to brighten ahead of the 6:30 sunrise. The race site is a place familiar to me, part of my usual turf, and I have even visited the site on the day of this very race - but today in the twilight it was truly transformed. Boats silently gathered in the water while the hushed transition area popped periodically with the hiss of tire pumps finishing their duties. I prepped my bike then found a spot to lie down, while my brothers made easy conversation. Everything stayed easy - breathe - and natural; we visited the bathroom, we made our way gently to the beach, we found a quiet spot on the grass to loosen up and suit up. I was comforted to have my big brother Jon by my side through the morning. Confident but quiet, Jon had years of experience with successful racing, including an event this distance, once so foreign to me, and now being shared.

Go time: I made my way to a place near the back of the sea of black wetsuits crammed into a chute, shuffling slowly toward the beach. I carried a bottle of water for washing down my last gel and sipping until the last minute. A man asked if he could have a little of my drinking water for his goggles, and helping him with this simple request reminded me of the way I feel about triathletes as a supportive community. Whatever bumping and nudging was about to occur in the lake would have more to do with a common goal than animosity. As a final bit of good fortune, just before entering the water I spotted Art - my mentor and coach - for a send-off embrace, and a great picture.

I was one of the last ones into the lake, which is where I wanted to be. Making it through this swim, for me, would be all about remaining calm. Easy does it. I sat in the water near the beach, at the back of the pack, just feeling the water slowly gliding around me. I was taking this pre-race opportunity to calm and center myself; the announcements and music faded from perception. Little did I know that because I lingered so near the shore, the start cannon was only about 10 feet to my right, and suddenly it exploded! The field splashed into action and the crowd erupted with noise; the stillness of the morning was over and I was excited. I was *in* this race - it was *real!*

And so I swam. I had never gone 2.4 miles in a row without a single stop, but I did what I was supposed to: swim easy, swim downhill, swim long, swim slowly - and it all came into place. I could hear the crowds on the shore, and see them lining each balcony of Monona Terrace. At one point, I spotted my family 5 stories above - they were displaying balloons and an enormous sign reading "Iron Man Dano." As I approached them, just for grins, mid-stroke I made a giant wave in their direction. With a field of more than 2,000 swimmers - in caps, goggles, and black wetsuits - I considered it a long shot that they would see me. They waved back! For a few little instants looking their way between strokes and breaths, I could see their tiny figures jumping around and clearly going crazy. Apparently my family and the people around them were also dumbfounded that they would pick me out of the arm-thrashing mob... looking back at the video they took, I was *really* wide and back.

I could hear the pro's names being announced exiting the water as I rounded the red buoy to head out for my second lap. By that time, I had brought myself in from the fringe, and was more comfortable being in the pack. I could sense the "toilet bowl effect" of everyone swimming together in a circle, though I wasn't able to get into a good draft. I was glad to be out there and feeling pretty good, apart from a slight headache from my mask being too tight. I took a few hits here and there, but nothing too serious, and soon came out of my zone and onto the land.

Just beyond the dock were the infamous wetsuit strippers. These early-morning volunteers are well-known for their role: they hang out by the swim exit and wait for athletes to come blasting out of the water, unzipping the top of their wetsuits before lying down on the ground for these volunteers to grab the wetsuit and yank it off! Note that course rules prohibit public nudity, so you have to be sure to wear something under the wetsuit to avoid embarrassing and costly surprises! Personally, I don't have a lot of trouble removing my wetsuit, but I considered it a kind of rite of passage, so I ran up, got on the ground, and let them have their way with me. It was good for me, and I think it was good for the two of them, too.

Usually, getting out of the lake I feel some degree of seasick, but today that degree was zero - I was fresh. Inside, I grabbed my transition bag, made my way to the "get naked room" and changed into biking clothes. Because I had a superstar-low number, I walked all the way down the rows and rows of bikes to mine at the end. I wanted to run, but my training book told me not to. It also told me I would *want* to run. One benefit of being a slow swimmer: it's really easy to find your bike. A volunteer called out my number on a megaphone as I approached; another volunteer had my bike unracked and ready for me. Throughout the day, the volunteer support was so much more than I ever imagined. Even at the back of the pack, I was a VIP.

I put on my cycling shoes, carefully clipped in, and headed down the helix to the bike course. As promised in my training books, the sensation of feeling better than I had in the last two months was absolutely true. I exercised great restraint as I got rolling, settled into my aerobars, and kept the pace easy. Living in the race-city and training on the race course itself made me very familiar with the bike course. It was a tremendous help - I knew all the terrain, road conditions, bumps, and turns. Along the way, I had a few nice conversations with fellow riders near my pace. I knew when to back off, when to go for it, and how to take the toughest descents with the least braking. On race day, it was funny to see the big piles of launched water bottles just beyond the bigger bumps.

The day was gorgeous and sunny, though the temperature climbed up to 85, and the midday heat was strong. I took my time at the water stops to refill my bottles, dump extra water on my back, and keep on eating. Indeed, as the miles went on, eating became less and less interesting although my need for fuel remained. Again, the volunteers were great. Justin from Endurance House was in Cross Plains, and refilled my bottles while I used the bathroom. The support simply made me feel elite. Police were at practically every intersection, roads were closed off, motorcycles cruised around with referees.

At one point, the pro men's field went zooming by me, finishing their second bike loop as I was finishing my first. I thought a car was coming up, but it was just their awesome disc wheels. Right after the first one passed me, I encountered my parents cheering, and shouted to them, "look, I'm in second place!" Shortly thereafter, a stream of other professionals blew by. I kept my excitement under control and rode steadily, so I could have plenty of energy to start the run. Coming into the home stretch of the bike course, my eyes saw physically what my mind had visualized countless times in the last year. The Madison skyline swept beyond the lake, and tears bubbled up again as they did throughout the day.

I was curious to see whether the marathon would feel anything like my practice transition runs... curious, to say the least, to discover whether my legs would run at all. As I stood to dismount, my quad began to cramp, so I bent my leg - and my hamstring began to cramp. Huh. But something about the dismount line approaching caused me to forget about that leg, and suddenly a volunteer took my bike and I was moving smoothly through T2. I found my brothers Jon and David on the other side; Jenn and Mom were also in the crowd as I came out of the chute (with a hat full of refreshing ice I had just picked up.) It felt better than I expected it to - partially because after six hours, my shoulders and butt were ready to get off that bike!

Just as the summaries say of Madison in the magazines, spectator support on the run course is unparalleled. People were everywhere, and really into it. As I began my marathon, top professionals were already completing the race and heading down the finish chute on the other side of the road. From there, anyone could be in front or behind me, because of the two-loop out-and-back course. I didn't care about my standings - I was just glad that my legs were off to a good start. I focused on my form and settled into the run. I walked through the water stations to take on nutrition, alternating sport drink and cola. In standalone marathons, I've done well with gels too, but the previous nine hours were catching up with me, and my stomach soon became my top limiter. This was not what I was expecting nor something I had experienced in training - I expected my legs to be burning up. So I regrouped a bit, walked until the gut-burn settled, then just kept trotting along.

When my guts were good, I moved forward at a steady pace - which I wasn't really expecting. I forgot to get the ibuprofen out of my special needs bag; I also refrained from using my last energy caffeine-bean because I suspected it might trigger a digestive meltdown. I adapted on the fly. The lap around the football field at Camp Randall was a thrill, even though the empty stadium was eerily quiet. I started singing a rousing "If you Wanna be a Badger," but it remained a solo. From time to time I crossed paths with friends, and was especially happy to run into Kelly, who was one of my very first teammates when this adventure all began. Her new yellow tires had defeated her biggest worry, and brought her flat-free to the run course to bring it home.

I was mentally prepared for the half-marathon turnaround, which is positioned only a half-block up the street from the finish line. Other much faster athletes ran ahead in celebration to the finish banner, and I quietly turned around a cone to begin one more half-marathon. *It's supposed to be hard.* People encouraging "you're almost there" probably didn't realize I still had about two hours to go. The sunset through the clear sky was gorgeous, and the air stayed mild into the night. The path became dark, and the way became quieter, but still I moved forward without a doubt. It was a test of patience and endurance, and the reward was a glorious finish.

The run down the finish chute was epic. Unbelievable. Even into the evening and night, fans stood all the way around the corner, two blocks long, several people deep, making it alive. Not competing for time or position, I remembered to look back and give way to a woman who went sprinting past (for whatever reason), and then slow down to slap some extended hands and soak up the moment. Finishing was my top goal, but I didn't want it to end. And then, there it was, the announcement I had heard in my mind and in my dreams, and now to all the world forever: "Dan Tyler - Madison - You are an Ironman! Way to go, Dan!"

A DAY-LONG SURPRISE PARTY

From before the dawn's early light began to soften the night's black sky, all through the morning and the heat of the day, and for hours after most of the city had gone to sleep, the fans cheered us on. They packed the shoreline until the 2 hour 20 minute swim cutoff, then continued to cheer until the last swimmer stepped onto land, in spite of being a moment too late to continue racing. They lined the bike course, particularly on the tougher climbs, accessible only by their own bikes or on foot. They lined the marathon course, standing on the sidewalk ringing cowbells, looking up from their books on campus, zipping along the course on their bikes to catch up with their favorite athlete, and relaxing in the sold-out cafes along State Street. From the first professional winning the race in under nine hours to the last amateur floating in in just under seventeen, music blared, lights shined, and an iconic voice announced each and every one of their accomplishments.

My own family's support was second to none. My parents drove in from Cleveland, my big brother flew in from Texas, my little brother from Georgia. They shared my final race-prep days with me: we toured the expo and the whole scene of the race that popped up suddenly, taking over the middle of town. They put up with my passionately specific requests related to nutrition, activity, and sleeping needs. While I was doing some of my own preparations, they secretly convened in the basement to solidify their own race-day plans.

They hand-made signs, sequentially broadcasting lyrics from my favorite motivational songs, slightly modified for the purpose of the day. They weren't flimsy, misspelled, or illegible, either - they were done right. Other athletes even asked me about them on the course, obviously getting their own motivation from them. One sign listed my favorite exclamation that Phil Liggett said of Lance after an impossibly excellent maneuver in the Tour: "he is such a star!" Another reminded me of one of my favorite race instructions: "Maintain task orientation." My family had created personalized T-shirts in the weeks before the race, and took orders among my friends. Racing was like showing up for a day-long surprise party, and 10,000 people were in on it.

The number of course volunteers far outweighed the number of athletes, and they treated every athlete like a professional. I've been to a few fancy places, and have received exceptional service from time to time; I've heard kind ovations from audiences of plays or speeches or music I've presented. But in day-to-day life, and certainly in the athletic arena, I've always just been an ordinary guy. Nobody rolls out a red carpet for me, nobody rises when I come into a room; I don't stay warm before my races in a special bus parked up near the starting line before the gun goes off. I may have some home-field advantage that helps me know where all the bathrooms are, but I don't feel entitled to going in front of anyone in line. The feeling on race day was much stronger than I had expected: I felt absolutely elite.

Inside of transition, athletes grab their bags then run into their sex-specific "get naked" rooms. In preparation, I had walked the transition routes the day before, to visualize how I would come into the building, turn down the right row, find my bag amidst all the other identical-looking bags (besides the green highlighting I put all over mine), then go through the correct door to the men's room. The visualization stopped there - I would go into *this* big room filled with white chairs, change my clothes as I had practiced, then go out *that* door, and walk *this* route to my bike on *this* rack. Though the physical layout was the same on race day, the scene looked different than it had in my head: all those white chairs were full, with dudes in all stages of nudity all over the place. No matter; I found a little space, sat down, and started digging into my bag.

As soon as I found a seat, a young man rushed up to me. He asked what he could do to help - I realized that this man was my personal attendant, at my beck and call for as long as it took to change my clothes and prepare for the long ride ahead. I wasn't even sure how to respond to this level of service: I stammered an apology for changing my shorts right in front of him, but he didn't bat an eye. I asked for a cup of water and suddenly it was in my hand. I asked him if he could find my sunglasses in the bag, and he found them, opened the case, and unfolded them. He un-velcro'd my shoes, then velcro'd them back when I changed my mind and said I'd prefer to carry them to the bike. All with calm, speed, and encouraging words along the way. When I got up to leave, he insisted on rolling up my wetsuit and putting away my swim gear for me.

Waiting outside were a row of gloved volunteers applying sunscreen wherever athletes asked for it; the rows of bikes were beyond. One benefit of being a slower swimmer is a much easier time finding your bike in transition. But instead of finding my bike racked as I left it, I found another volunteer standing at the end of the rack, with my bike in hand, pointed toward the exit and ready to roll, as if holding the President's limo door open. Out on the bike course when I pulled into an aid station and began to dismount and look for a tree to lean my bike against while I spent a minute in the bathroom, volunteers rushed up to me, and not only held my bike, but asked me which drinks I'd like them to refill my water bottles with. This treatment made me feel appreciated beyond what I ever expected or even felt I deserved; it validated the magnitude of the race.

People I have never seen before in my life shouted out to

me like I was in the lead at a world championship. The huge crowds on the climbs reminded me of scenes from the Tour de France. Volunteers at every station raced to my aid like I was the record-holder and they were clamoring for the opportunity to be near me. I knew my family would be on the course and looking for me, but everyone else also seemed to treat me with the kind of love befitting of their son, brother, or partner.

When you make up your mind to achieve a goal and focus on it intently for a year, then see it unfolding right in front of you, you can forget that other people don't see it the same way. They can't believe I'm doing what I'm doing, they say. In terms of the figure of speech, *I can't believe it* either. But in my heart, that's exactly what I've been doing all year: believing in it. That's what made it possible. They can't believe it, because they're only seeing a snapshot of the result of all the effort. They might imagine the intensity or volume that goes into training, or the effort that goes into the day. But as I go by and hear "I could never do that," I respectfully disagree. *Yes you could*, I think - you could do it, if you believed you could. And you worked hard to get it, of course.

When I reflect back on race day, I remember feeling dumbfounded at the level of support. I wondered: for what? What did I do to merit this kind of encouragement and accolade? Apparently these volunteers didn't know I wasn't cool in high school and wasn't desired on any sports teams. Who I used to be had become irrelevant in favor of what I had become by entering this race. It was hard to understand that on this one day, by stepping into this race, I had become something different, I had earned a new rank.

I think also that without knowing it by name, in my reflections back on this race and its transformative power, I was practicing gratitude. Prior to the race, my visualizations of the course contained roads, hills, and landscapes; after the race, my memories were vibrant with the colorful, dynamic din of all the various people. Keeping my fond memories focused on the support has helped me remain grateful for all those people who made the race-day experience what it was, and challenged me to focus my own racing career on inclusiveness, support, joy, and generosity.

After the 112-mile bike ride is over, you run a marathon. "And *then* you run a marathon" - a phrase that still makes me shake my head with stupefied awe. The marathon is a beautiful and challenging distance all on its own, let alone as part of a larger race. As I ran and the day gave way to evening, the intensity and noise gave way to some quieter moments. Seconds became minutes of no sound but one foot stepping after another. The sun set. Sometimes I welcomed the solitude, as I fatigued and found less strength to smile back at those smiling at me. There wasn't anything remarkable about it. But every mile or so, there was an oasis of light, music, food, and friendly people to re-energize me on my weary way.

I remember the moment of my own firm decision to sign up, standing down by the lake, in the dark and rain of an evening thunderstorm. It was one year before - and I was volunteering as a course-marshal to help be sure athletes stayed on course as the road gave way to the dark, gravel lakeside path. I offered all the support one person could give to another making their way through the night. Little did I know that my sense of empathy would begin to spill over the boundaries of the race setting, or that I would experience the ultimate empathy by completing the very same event a year later.

PRESENCE AND THE TRANSFORMATION

Of all the time I've wasted regretting what I might have done in the past, and worrying about what I may have to deal with in the future, on race day, I spent 14 hours and 11 minutes right where I was. No regrets, no judgments, no worries - just the moment, and all the capabilities I had given myself to celebrate it. Why worry? I figured out what I needed to do, made my plan, and did the work. I stuck with my own goals and ideals throughout. There's no substitute for putting in the training hours, and I had certainly paid my dues. There was no reason to dwell on the possibility of failure, because the very task at hand was the success in itself.

Let's face it, 14 hours in a row is a long time to do anything - especially physical work. Without possibly knowing how I would feel as the day went on, I set out with a mindset of gradual forward progress, settling into a slow and steady burn, focusing on my fuel economy, as it were. If I thought about the distant finish line - if I even thought about the transition to the next sport - I could become mired with impatience and feel that I was getting nowhere. After all, I had spent the whole year looking forward to this day - why would I want it to be over? My focus remained not on how far I had traveled or how far I had yet to go, but how I was traveling at the moment.

Swimming, for example, comes down to the art of form, carefully and intentionally sliding the body through a medium 1,000 times denser than air, and unforgiving of errant movements. Good fitness and strong muscles are important, but mechanical form is pinnacle for a hydrodynamic vessel - which requires consistent focus. My training goal has not been trying to swim particularly fast, but swimming as efficiently as possible, trying to feel myself nicely gliding through the water rather than fighting this heavy liquid. What does it feel like to be a dolphin? I bet it feels relaxed in the water. As I turn my attention to a certain elegance in the water, anxiety dissolves.

If someone asks me what I think about while swimming 2.4 miles, for more than an hour in a lake where the bottom is far from visible, I can say only that I think about, well, swimming. There's only one thing worth thinking about at the moment, and that's the quality of each stroke... and a quick look at the buoy from time to time to be sure I'm still going the right direction. Repetitive though it may seem, there are enough intricate movements happening with each turn of the arms to completely occupy the mind. When I've felt the hot rush of panic during race-swims, focusing intently on the mechanics has been the most reliable way to come back to control.

Feeling the smooth water gently flowing over a slippery body sounds great in theory, but what about the 2,000 other swimmers all around, starting from the same line at the same starting cannon, creating an audible din with their splashes and bubbly mess of bodies? Often I hear stories of people reluctant to attempt triathlon because they are apprehensive about swimming, especially in a mass of other swimmers. Many triathletes tell horror stories of being kicked in the face, smacked in the head, or pushed underwater in the herd. For me, the experience has been different perhaps because my approach to swimming has focused almost entirely on being calm and relaxed in the water. I also won't discredit the simple truth that in the back of the pack where I swim, there are simply fewer people.

My inward focus in swimming allowed me to easily change

the way I reacted to the other athletes. We were all making our way through the same course, and each using some kind of personal strategy to manage our reactions to the water itself; after all, we are all humans. I considered it unlikely that anyone next to me had a personal vendetta against me in trying to move from 1,917th to 1,916th place with another 13 hours of racing still to go. These ideas helped me keep my perspective when I did periodically get smacked in the head.

I am tough enough to do this race after all, and the guy probably didn't mean to do it. For that matter, it could even be a girl, and a lot of triathlete women are quite good-looking, particularly in swimsuits, so wouldn't it be some kind of dream come true to be this close to one? Gimmicks maybe, but the mental tricks helped me keep my head down, keep my cool, and keep swimming my own swim.

Once I eventually did come out of the water, a huge hurdle was behind me. I was glad to be on land again, and had no desire to look back and analyze the swim. In the moment, I was making my way to my bike. I was heeding the advice I had read about really taking it easy as I transitioned from a long time in a horizontal position to a long time in a vertical one, even though I felt really good. And why rush, during these few hundred feet that were lined with spectators, several deep and cheering like mad? I tried to strike a balance between being in my own zone carefully executing my plan, and also being sure to enjoy the excitement of the day, which dramatically energized me. It was an effort to do everything deliberately, to not miss a moment, to love every bit of it.

Throughout the day, I felt a strange, surreal feeling of disconnection from years of watching and hearing about this race, and my own self *being* the person in the race - a sort of disbelief. A confluence of the image of the race in my mind, the words I had written about it, and the simple reality of my actually being part of it. I had taken on the challenge, worked hard, trained diligently for a long time, memorized the course, procured equipment, and executed my plan. I was focused on doing my best, in a race only between myself and the clock. It was motivating to hear my friends' encouragement and even pride as I trained, but I had completely overlooked the input I would get on race day itself. To me, I had spent the season as an ordinary guy training carefully to do something hard. Once race day came, people started treating me like a superstar, like I was a professional, a VIP.

The athletic effort wasn't terribly different than a super-long training day (or series of days) but was energized by literally thousands of fans all along the course. When I visualized the course, I had thought about the route, the hills, the equipment, the nutrition - and honestly hadn't considered that anyone would be out there to watch it, except perhaps in certain central locations. I traveled over the same course I knew so well, but layers of life had been added. I couldn't get enough of it. On the run, by the setting sun, groups of people still cheered.

In my visualization of the course, I was prepared for a long test of my own endurance ("Dano à Dano"), just as I had practiced on my long solo training sessions. I had prepared to keep pursuing my goal, to keep believing in myself; I wasn't expecting people I had never met to also be believing in me. Who was I to be called athlete, inspiration … hero? I knew my own experience as a volunteer, but I hadn't put together a picture of what I would encounter from the inside, from the athlete's point of view. Kayakers along the swim course before dawn to medics at the finish line past midnight.

I was never in it for fame. Yes, I had hoped that my effort might in some way inspire people, but hadn't given a lot of thought to what that might look like. The VIP treatment from volunteers on the course transformed a long, challenging route into a major event - they gave the day the personality that wouldn't be present even if I achieved the whole distance again, but on my own. This may have been one of the greatest impressions the race made on me: I was the guy on the receiving end of all the excitement, and being the focal point of this accolade was part of the transformation - the coronation, as it were - to the permanent title, the state of being called "an

Ironman."

Visualization is the practice of setting a particular scene in the mind, then placing yourself into it and looking around from that perspective. Inspecting from within, visualization is a sort of meditation on the race. In most races, triathletes can gain time and smoothness by understanding how the course is physically put together - there's nothing more frustrating than feeling great, running out of the transition, and having to stop to find out which way to turn next!

Because I was participating in my hometown race, I had the advantage of training on the race course itself, and had many opportunities to visualize my race day with great precision. I knew exactly what many of the scenes looked like from seeing them with my own eyes, around town, over and over. Visualization is mental training as well: as I focused on situations, I framed them with peace, confidence, and strength. I practiced my race-day feelings. Sometimes I even set the mental scene with something from my list of worries, then visualized myself making whatever repair or adaptation was required to successfully solve the problem.

Once race day arrived, there was nowhere to be but the moment. Looking away into the future would be foolish because I had spent so long waiting for this very day - I practically had nothing else beyond it. Why waste energy speculating on something fictitious when there was so much race-day goodness to take in? Truly, my whole race plan from its very beginning addressed my worries and needs. I had the right equipment, backups, and risk management. I had my own self to be accountable to, and I knew exactly what I had put into my preparation. I had faith in my own abilities because I had created them from the ground up over the course of the year; when I considered what I'd done, I had proof.

Out of the physical conditioning, the mental visualizations, the excitement of the atmosphere, and wide-open eyes taking in each moment for what it was, the very dimensions of "reality" expanded. As I discovered myself on race day in the exact spot that I had set my visualization scene, seeing the same things but finally living the moment I had been anticipating, being in that moment was far larger than "real." I was overwhelmed to be living in moments on race day somehow spanning the entire period of training, of dreaming; culminating the season with the entire season itself rolled up into that instant. To call the day "surreal" would barely scratch the surface - in a way that I don't expect to ever be able to adequately describe, the day began to explain infinity.

PART II
FOR SOMETHING GREATER

GENESIS

I first tried to make running a hobby while living in Omaha back in 2002. I graduated from college and moved a thousand miles west, on my own with a new full-time job and no local friends. Running seemed like the kind of thing that people in that situation do. Running is a simple thing: everyone has some shorts and some athletic shoes, it's easy to do solo, and there are plenty of places to go out and just run. Funny, I sure did feel awkward.

A couple times a week I went out on the sidewalk and ran around town a bit, then came back. When I traveled for work, I took my shoes along and set out from the hotel. I wanted it to be a hobby. Training plans were a completely foreign concept, as were the running-magazines in which many of them were written. When my coworkers invited me to join them at a local 10k, I showed up grossly overdressed and stashed my sweats in some bushes. But I had a fun time, and felt a great sense of accomplishment from finishing a 10k.

I thought I would meet people running, but I never plugged into any group runs or clubs - I didn't even know they existed - and found myself always running alone. I now know a lot of people who love the solitude of running by themselves, but back then I was in a stage of my life when I didn't know anyone and *always* felt solitary, and yearned for activities that would help me connect. I certainly didn't feel confident enough to make "want to go for a run?" an easy invitation to get to know someone new, especially a girl!

My running had no strategy or plan; I do not recall feeling like I was very good. I had a pair of legitimate running shoes, but unbeknownst to me they were too big and not even laced right. They probably came from a shoe store in the mall, without anyone advising me that shoes and people have individual matchmaking needs. I did stick with it - a little bit of unstructured running here and there as the construction company moved me from Omaha to New York to Tampa, then as I moved myself to Wisconsin.

I tried to use running as a release: a break from long hours at work and an invigorating jolt to my heart rate to feel energized, and a nice way to explore my changing surroundings. I wanted to be a person who was "in shape." But it just was not a part of me.

The best thing that happened was losing my job.

In the summer of 2007 I lived in Wisconsin and worked in the business of managing design for new indoor water parks. Until 4:30 one Tuesday afternoon, when my boss called me in to his office to tell me that I - and another 30 percent of the company - wasn't welcome to come back in the morning. I was blindsided, although looking back, there were significant structural flaws in the company's way of doing business and the writing was on the wall. I found myself in my car on the way home, with a simple box of cleaned-out desk-things, and a mind wide open in the sudden absence of any professional obligation to that firm, or those projects into which I had invested so much emotion.

The job hadn't been very fun for months, and I had considered leaving but wasn't sure where to go or what to do next. Left to my own status quo, I wouldn't have dared to leave one certain thing without another to go to - but the layoff was my permission to be free. What I did outside of the work day was all mine; it just took a much larger period "outside of the work day" for me to finally launch my endurance adventure. It was my push off the ledge, gingerly expecting that I would find a soft landing at some point, but with nothing to do in the mean time but go for a ride.

When the sun rose Wednesday morning and the alarm clock did not go off, I woke up and had breakfast, then went out for a bike ride. With all the time in the world on my first day of unemployment, my ride was a bit longer than usual - a wide loop all the way around Madison on the Capitol City Trail. 20 miles felt like a huge accomplishment! When I got home, I showered and looked for jobs. The next day - same thing. Friday - again. Even with a pretty good resume and connections in town, it takes a long time to find a job with the right fit. I was eager to get paid again, but not desperate or wanting to begin a new job that was destined to be lousy. As days passed, so did the miles around the Capitol City trail. I didn't know any other bike routes, and wasn't yet familiar with the concept of road-riding, so I rode nearly 1,000 miles in loops around the city.

My confidence as a rider increased. When August came around, I entered my first organized event: a 100-mile charity ride. A *century* ride! I made painstaking preparations, washing my bike and packing enough food into my jersey for the whole 100 miles, not realizing that extensive rest stops with food and drinks would be set up along the way. Sometimes I referred to it as a "race," which usually yielded a correction by the person unfortunate enough to endure my over-zealous anticipation. On "race day," I rushed through the rest stops where hundreds of other riders milled around and relaxed with the bands: I thought I was supposed to keep on riding hard toward that finish line!

Especially after a couple months of being out of work, where each day's stigmatic cloud of "unemployment" hung over my head and suggested that I should doubt my self-worth, going the distance was a big milestone for me. I was pleased to have accomplished this challenge as a result of time well-spent in preparation. Reaching 100 miles did not require other people, it didn't take bosses or performance reviews or even salaries: it just took me and my determination. Next, I wanted to learn to run. I guess that's how it started.

At some point that fall, I received a flyer with purple and green logos and a list of marathons in fun locations. Curiously, it was a flyer I had received once before when I lived alone in Omaha, but never gave a second thought. *I'm not an athlete, I'm busy with work, I could never do that kind of thing* - excuses that now I hear people say all the time.

What made my life so different in the fall of 2007 when that purple and green post card arrived and I actually went to an informational meeting, from 2002 when I really could have used motivation and even one new friend? When life shook me up and handed me extra space to try something intriguing, I went for it. Something about the feeling of transition from losing a job combined with the confidence of finishing a 100-mile bike ride pushed me to follow my curiosity, rather than dismiss myself as ineligible, as "not an athlete." When I first moved out on my own in 2002, I had the excitement of starting a new job and building a place for myself; five years later I suddenly had a new perspective on what was given to me from outside and what I made for myself.

TO FIND A TEAM

The external factors - both the ones that motivate and the ones that aggravate - all come and go as life moves along; the truest teacher that will always remain is the one in the mirror. This is clear to me now, but has not always been. The values that most fundamentally define our lives must come from within, but at some point of genesis, begin with a nudge. An object at rest will remain at rest unless someone invites them out for a run.

I have to take each step in training and racing - no one else can do it for me - but the sport couldn't survive and grow without training buddies. Friends who invite friends to join them for a run; coworkers who invite each other to participate in a health-improving program; teammates who band together to take on a certain challenge; families who dare each other to complete a race together. Even consistency itself is a great motivator: "I like this class and I try to go every week," or "I make running with this group a regular part of my schedule."

If you've been reluctant to try something new and just can't seem to get yourself to do it, perhaps you could grab on to someone or something else to help you get started. Maybe you know someone else who is similarly tentative, and your combined desire to go at it pushes you past the tipping point. New year's resolutions can be very effective, but there's no need to wait for another new year.

I don't always feel like diving into my workouts, but when I finish I'm almost always glad I did: recruiting a co-conspirator goes a long way toward sticking with a commitment. It's not cheating to seek a little motivation; the greater disappointment would be giving up. And from my perspective, it's certainly not burdensome. On the contrary - I'm grateful for everyone who has ever asked: *"want to join me for a run?"*

These same phenomena occur when charity athletes put a mission and a group of teammates behind their training. You've heard motivating stories of people who have survived near-death encounters and come back to achieve great things, so ask yourself: why wait? Let a day or an event, or maybe someone who wants to team up with you, supplement your internal desire and make you even more motivated to move toward your goals.

When I found Team In Training, all it took was a little nudge to get through the door at the informational meeting, and the rest took care of itself. I never set out to be any kind of great runner, but it wouldn't matter so much when I focused instead on the charity's mission. Almost none of the people involved are professional athletes; in fact, most are novices. Many of them aren't very concerned about the clock, but each one's participation supports a purpose - to save lives. Most also run for a second purpose - to go the distance for themselves.

Team In Training is a nonprofit group that combines endurance sports like marathons, triathlons, and century bike rides with the charitable cause of supporting the Leukemia and Lymphoma Society. Volunteers who take on these athletic events are supported with coaching, schedules, and new friends at regular group training sessions. They train for several months, building up together for a significant race. In exchange, they raise money for the cause. It's straightforward, and very powerful.

When I arrived at the meeting, I was warmly welcomed, and the promotional videos struck a ringing chord with me. This was a group with a positive energy, ready to accept a rookie like me. It was structured to teach me everything about running that I never was able to figure out on my own, in an environment that wasn't judgmental of such ignorance. Instead of a stereotypical group of stoic hard-core athletes, this was a heart-felt group made up of all types, ready to train hard, but also willing to open up and cry when joy or sorrow merited it. Why hold back emotions that are real and true?

Much like my efforts in years past, I started with a 20-minute run; it was a slow lap around my brother's apartment complex. But this time, it was the distance I was *supposed* to run, and it was followed with another similar run two days later, as prescribed by my Coach. It didn't feel great, and I went on to discover various new sensations in my shins, knees, and hips, but I showed up each time my team met.

With the various pains and fatigue, it wasn't always easy to appreciate the gains adding up in training, but raising money in parallel made the gains more tangible. Reaching out to so many people, seeking donations, also created a new layer of commitment, because each person I told of my goals was another reason to achieve them. I was surprised to discover that people actually read my blog updates and showed interest in what I was doing; there's something exciting about the challenge of training for a significant event that encourages others to come along for the ride. I pinned their notes of support on my wall as a reminder that people believed in what I was doing. It wasn't because I was training to run a half-marathon, it was because I had connected my effort with something greater.

As the fall gave way to winter, the miles increased while temperatures decreased. Before I came to Wisconsin, the winter temperature might have included a qualifier of "Fahrenheit" or "Celsius" - here the number is often clarified with "above" or "below." In a season when many solo runners give up, the sun rose over our group's dedicated footsteps, the air crisp and the visibility endless. In the morning before the bustle begins, things are quiet, as people - and animals - stay inside their warm homes: it's a setting for clarity.

On mornings like these, it's best to have a team. Friends who you are looking forward to sharing stories with, and coaches who are expecting your attendance; a goal-race that's getting closer each day and a training plan that needs you to get out the door and put in the miles in time to be ready. But even more, approaching endurance events in a mission-driven context adds more motivation for getting out the door, and the cause itself helps keep everything in perspective.

Someone who gets up in the morning - someone is doing it right now - to endure a chemotherapy treatment is having a lot less fun than someone getting up to go running, no matter how cold or windy. That person needs us. When I felt uncomfortable running, I reminded myself "this is easier than chemo." Putting a challenge like a half-marathon right next to something like cancer makes the very ability to run appear a brighter blessing.

At the end of the season, I went to Phoenix to run my first half-marathon. I learned that the collective group of 3,000 Team In Training runners and walkers from around the country, in that event alone, raised 3.6 *million* dollars. Suddenly it was clear in a new way: that's the kind of accomplishment that comes from serious, selfless dedication. This team creates friendships locally while training, and nationally during events; it fills up the streets with runners and lines them with appreciative fans. I crossed the finish line feeling like I had not just become a runner, but had become part of a community.

Running in this context is not solitary, but stands for solidarity. Here, coaches and mentors believe in participants more than they know, and embody the ideals of support when people need it most. Champions here are defined by their intentions and welcomed for their effort, and ultimately rewarded: ordinary people can dream about a finish line and wake up with a medal around their neck. Here, running takes on a whole new meaning, full and important, connected in symbolism to a cause.

RACE REPORT:
MARDI GRAS MARATHON

In February of 2010, I kicked off my third year with Team In Training with a trip to New Orleans to run my fourth marathon. I had entered my third season as a runner, the first one where I finally felt like I "enjoyed" running, and where I felt ready to push it a little harder. I went to New Orleans with a secret desire to find my edge and achieve my best time, without giving up the parts that made me enjoy the sport. I left with one of my most meaningful race experiences, seeing how over the course of four months, our team became a family.

This marathon would be a challenging mental battle between wanting to do something that I believed was possible if I really worked hard - finish under four hours - and wanting to spend the whole day - running included - with my teammates. For most of the season, my top priorities were to be a good teammate and mentor, stay healthy, and train smart to become a better runner. Simple as that. On the cold and snowy Saturday team long runs, I ran whatever pace allowed me to spend time with my teammates. On weeknights I added some hills and tempo work solo to make myself stronger. It wasn't until the morning of our 16-mile training run that I took off with the "speedy" runner group, mostly because I wanted a chance to get to know them a little better. From there, though, something clicked and told me *wow: you can be a "speedy" runner*!

So I arrived in New Orleans with a secret pace card showing a series of negative splits adding up to a 3:58 finish. My plan was to spend the weekend with my friends, corral up with my "speedy" gang and get started together, and see how I felt as the race unfolded. (Coach Art explained that he would start in the "OK Corral").

I have such mixed emotions about speed that I feel guilty even writing about a time goal - my race reports aren't about my splits and speeds. I'm not going to boast about my time or compare it to anyone else's. I'm not going to win a marathon. That's not why I'm here. I'm not going to suggest that my goals should be yours or vice versa. I just want to run with the Team, run for joy, and keep challenging myself because I don't ever want apathy to replace the excitement I have for the sport.

The race began, music blared, and an extremely-exuberant announcer screamed "this is not a drill!" in a tone befitting a monster-truck rally. My teammates helped each other hang on to the reins as we got going steadily but gently. At mile 5, our pace was steady and I was feeling healthy and positive. The sun had come up and the air was warming; it felt so good to switch from training in the snow to racing in shorts and a tank top.

Getting ready to make a turn and run through Audubon Park, my group came apart a bit at a water station. As I waited for the others, I felt a pull beckoning me to make my first negative split, even if it meant making it on my own. This was my day and I had to go for it: I hated to leave my friends, but I had to try something crazy. And so began the hardest marathon I could have set out for myself.

There is a thin gray line between personal best and complete disaster. A runner's best marathon requires a careful blend of energy output and conservation, having the discipline to finish with everything depleted, but not a moment before. The amount varies by person, by training, and by the day. As the miles went by, I experienced waves of doubt and confidence. I stayed grounded by taking in nutrition, doing what I had practiced, and simply putting one foot in front of the other. My mind and burning legs incessantly asked the questions: *can we make it, do we have to stop?* Some other part of my consciousness replied *no - at least not right now; you can keep going for another moment.* Then another.

I entered the "bite me zone," a sensation that many runners experience in the late miles of a marathon: a period of extreme grumpiness where they wonder why the heck they signed up for this stupid race to begin with. Somehow, knowing that these unusual emotions are part of the typical race experience helped me notice them with curiosity from some mysterious place slightly outside myself, rather than become consumed by them and break down.

Suddenly, from my mystical mental marathon world I was pulled back to the road in front of me as a voice called my name and a Team In Training coach began to run beside me. He was from a chapter in another state, and I had never met him before, but he raised my spirits out of my slump. He helped me keep up my faith, and we talked about the parallel seasons we had had with our respective teams, pursuing common goals in spite of not knowing each other. He was right there when I needed him the most.

I tried to return the favor. The next couple miles, 23 and 24, were an out-and-back, so I watched for other purple shirts and called out to them as they passed. I shouted "Go Team!" to each of them. Most seemed to snap out of a funk similar to mine, and respond. I saw my teammate Mike, who shouted "Dano, you're a madman!" - which was the best thing he could possibly have said to me. Indeed, it was true: my mind had gone to a place far away from its ordinary patterns. I saw my four other "speedy" buddies and was enthused to see them together and still making great progress. Pursuing my own goal wasn't quite as mutually exclusive with being a good teammate as I had thought.

In the late miles, things happen very slowly, and they can change drastically as well. The marathon takes you to your edge in many respects, where you are very fragile. After the out-and-back section ended, things became very quiet. It's not that the high-fives and *Go Team*'s of moments ago didn't count, but they didn't last. Again, suddenly, I found myself accompanied by a coach - this time, my own coach, Art. With him at my side, all of a sudden I was a world-record holder, a Kenyan! The nerve - he started to videotape me, which was a lot of fun, until I spontaneously burst into tears. Go figure. Art said he'd run with me as long as I wanted, which was a great assurance, but didn't feel fair to the others, considering just how critical the coaches had been to me. We made one turn where I figured he'd leave, but he didn't. That was really good. He said he'd run me all the way to the finish if I wanted.

I left Coach Art with a couple miles to go, to finish it off. Just a couple miles to keep hanging in there at my best pace, at the edge of my breaking point. Finally, there was the 26-mile banner. I had made it! I started to feel pretty good, then the fans picked up again, then I started to feel great, then I saw the finish chute, and I was a new man. I straightened up my outfit and number, looked back to let any sprinting people go past (one did), and stood up tall into my best form to smile at the crowd and - hands up - get my finish photo! All morning I had wanted to enjoy the day, but was also dying to be finished. Now I couldn't believe that I was, and I had made my goal to boot. I was tougher than the marathon that day, I had put in the hard work and earned the reward.

From there, it was gently stretching, slowly starting to eat again, and walking funny. At the TNT tent I received the much-coveted 26.2 pin, and then did the only thing that seemed right to do next: I went back to the finish chute to cheer in my teammates. When I broke from my "speedy" friends to run a faster pace back at mile 5, I felt like I was leaving them - but indeed I wasn't. We shared the same course, reunited at the finish line, and then returned to the finish chute again. As the end of the race grew nearer and other racers headed home, team Wisconsin stayed. Our walker was still on the course, and we wanted to welcome her home as well.

Most runners were gone, the band packed up, and most of the fans went home. The Kenyans were certainly showered and resting as the last remaining participants came walking or running in. As the end of the race drew near, the gates that once held fans out of the way were pulled aside so the few of us remaining could make a human receiving line at the finish, giving each finisher a hero's welcome. After all, each one of them had finished the marathon, all 26.2 miles, just like me. After a long pause, in an incredible moment, the last Team In Training participant appeared. Around her was a parade of every coach and staff member who had been out on the course, bringing her in. I had never before stayed at a race until the last person crossed the line, but today for me and for Team Wisconsin, it was the only thing in the world that we needed to do. No one was left behind.

New Orleans was rife with symbolism. Along the course, the scars of hurricane Katrina still appeared in a mostly-rebuilt city, like a wall still bearing a spray-painted "1 dead in attic." However, mixed in with dilapidation were well-maintained homes; both of these types had residents in the windows and on the porches waving and shouting encouragement. I thought about the local jazz funeral tradition, beginning with a solemn march to the cemetery but shifting to the "second line" parade of hopeful, boisterous music as the crowd leaves the place.

I noticed how this parallels Team In Training, whose members often live close to the unbearable sadness of cancer's impacts, but who find strength and positive spirit in helping each other experience joy in their athletic pursuits. When the national TNT group assembled its 700 members on race morning, a brass band led us from our hotel to the starting line, as we waved purple handkerchiefs and other racers looked down from their hotel rooms. I noticed how it even parallels the marathon itself, in my experience of taking myself into a very painful place, for the experience of enduring and the joyful relief of finishing. After the pain and grief, which does require and deserve space and time, eventually comes hope.

The juxtaposition can be stunning. Spending four hours

pursuing a goal on the edge of my ability, barely believing that I'll make it, and then suddenly standing still and receiving a medal. The sudden clarity of all that I've been anticipating in the moment that it is actually achieved. The morning after the race, I watched the team bus depart and was struck with a sinking, painful heartache, like watching something dear slip away, with no idea what to do next. I knew I had willingly put all my whole heart into this team, allowing it to wash over and consume me, and my reward was unbridled, true joy; perhaps you could call it true love. The most exceptional experiences in life begin with the willingness to dive completely into them with reckless abandon, understanding that some day, like everything in life, they will have to come to an end.

Upstairs, my roommate had checked out, and the hotel room was lighted only by the 28th floor window, from a drizzly gray New Orleans cityscape. For the first time in three days, my mind began to revert to its habits, suggesting any number of tasks that I could jump into, the next projects that I could begin. But the feeling of "it's over" was so overwhelming that I was paralyzed more by the weekend's conclusion than the soreness in my legs. So I slowly packed up my things - removing TNT finishers' pins from my shirt, disconnecting my race number, cleaning off my shoes. Usually I'm eager to sit down and write a race report; this time I knew I would need a little extra time before I could put my feet on the ground enough to make sense of it. The next couple days would be like the New Orleans-style funeral, with sad goodbyes eventually giving way to a big brass band celebrating all that has been good about what was shared together. The sadness makes clear just how deeply I've been moved.

The morning after the race, my teammates and I ate beignets for breakfast at the famous Café du Monde, overlooking the sunrise over the foot of the Mississippi. I recalled my trip to its headwaters the previous summer - a cold trickling stream a thousand miles away. So too had my team built momentum on its course toward New Orleans, becoming something much mightier than each individual who joined it.

And not only had the "speedy" five become close friends, and the whole Wisconsin group rallied at the finish line, but about 700 Team members from around the country also completed the race with us, and collectively raised over 1.1 million dollars. My pursuit of my personal goal turned out not to be selfish, but achievable because of the magnanimous current. Although with the race's conclusion I felt adrift in the ocean, I was confident that I had evolved, and could thrive upon it.

SOME DAYS YOU RACE,
SOME DAYS YOU MAKE RACES HAPPEN

My favorite water station at Ironman Wisconsin was on Walnut street, as it passed under the railroad bridge near the power plant, halfway through the two-loop out-and-back course. Four times I ran through this water station, staffed by volunteers from Team In Training, and each time I was rejuvenated with hugs, big high-fives, and even a couple of solid chest-bumps. As I rounded the corner to come into the station the first time, I connected with a friend whose father had passed away from blood cancer, and I was reminded that the kind of support this charity team gives its members goes far beyond one day at the races. The station was stocked with water, bananas, crackers, pretzels, sponges, and more, but those weren't what gave me energy.

Picture it: a row of tables, covered with thousands of cups - far more than you could ever consume. A racer coming up to it can find relief in grabbing one and drinking it. The stuff on the table provides the liquid, calories and nutrition metabolized by the body into motion. But the real race-side water stop does so much more than that: it gives spirit, hope and life back to athletes who are wearing down, beginning to doubt, feeling the pain of a journey too hard to complete alone. The water itself can soothe the body and even the mind, but it doesn't do so much for the soul.

It's the smile at the end of the arm holding out the water, the cowbells, the music, the shouts of encouragement, someone calling out your name and telling you to keep going - even if they just read it from your race bib. It's person after person, all along the course, singling you out and telling you that you're doing something important, you're achieving a tremendous goal. They're telling you the thing you spent so much time working toward is valid and meaningful, and you're going to achieve it.

Working to support racers is an important duty for all racers to take on at some point, and can be just as gratifying as running a race, if you let it. After all, how much harder - if not impossible for some - would a marathon (or any event) be without course support? Even in the high-priced, highly-produced races, those supporters are volunteers. Some of them are experienced, while some have never raced. Some show up a bit indifferent or begrudgingly in the early morning, perhaps dragged by a friend, and some are excited to be part of the fun; morning sleepiness quickly gives way to intensity as the sun emerges. I bet many of those volunteers get inspired - and I'd venture a guess that a day at the races often plants curious seeds in minds that sprout into a determined pair of shoes and a leap-of-faith jog around the neighborhood. Consider it karma, call it what you will, but make time to show up on the other side of the table, to create the energy each race needs, for the sake of the sport. You'll allow the cycle to remain sustainable. Some days you race, some days you make races happen.

Of course, not everyone volunteering at the race believes in the race or has trained for and focused on the race as much as the participants. But they show up nonetheless, and give the racers their attention. In our ordinary days, countless strangers pass anonymously by, unnoticed altogether; if they happen to do something we don't expect we might get annoyed or judge them. At the water stop, volunteers support the racers whether the volunteers themselves are racers or not - or whether they even value the race in the same way as the participants. Judgment gets suspended for the sake of support. In spite of periodic incredulous utterances like "I could never do that," the volunteers nonetheless extend a vital hand with sustenance. When we pass others in the course of our ordinary lives, and we see them going through experiences far different from ours, how do we treat them - and what can we learn from the water stop?

Without even knowing it, some of the people with whom we interact are in need of some kind of water stop. They may be moving through a dark patch, desperate for the next oasis of light and life, wherever it may be. We understand it within the context of the races: why should it be any different any other day? Why only support a stranger in the night 17 hours a year, when they may be struggling through a much harder journey? I worked hard at that race for more than 14 hours - it was a long day, and it was tough. But after I finished, I got a medal, ate hot pizza, went home and took a shower and went to bed, and when I woke up in the morning it was all over. There are others I know - and countless others I never will - who struggle through one evening only to wake up the next morning to the same heartaches or body aches. People with degenerative illnesses, lost jobs, or broken relationships try to stand up tall and move forward, trying not to let on just how fragile their journey has really become.

I have become much stronger through all the training I've done. I've become tougher and more determined. Determined *to do what*, I ask myself, outside of racing? Because truly, athletic fitness is only one element of a truly healthy life - a life in balance. Racing supplements the "rest of life" - but what is it that makes up this "rest of life" and how can race experiences extend into it? My neighbor had Parkinson's disease. There's no cure, and every morning, in spite of his positive attitude, he faced another day to endure. Whenever we talked, he asked me about my latest races - he was eager to hear my updates, and offered a lot of encouragement. He didn't have to ask me to mow his lawn and shovel his sidewalk; I'm the guy for the job, after all - I'm in great shape from all the training. Why put all that effort into being good at racing if it's only for racing's sake?

Imagine how many countless others in our lives could use some race-day encouragement, even for a single moment. Who might snap out of a downward streak and regain the strength to make it to some sort of finish line? I often consider this important lesson from racing: *how can I be the hand holding out the water?*

ESSENTIAL INPUT FROM THE
BENEVOLENT OBSERVER

Through training and racing, you get to know yourself. You learn about your abilities, likes and preferences, strengths and weaknesses. You identify and hone in on areas for focus - whether it's celebrating and capitalizing on strengths, or targeting and improving weaknesses. Surprisingly though, sometimes the issues aren't evident to you; sometimes things are completely different than they appear! Here's where others enter the picture, if you're willing to listen to them: they are a source of feedback from an entirely different vantage point. From inside and out, feedback is essential to improvement. Sometimes a simple positive hand is the very gesture that enables someone's healthy lifestyle.

Set a scene in the far lap lane of a municipal pool, in the summer evening quiet after all the screaming kids have gone. I'm accompanied by a long time friend and teammate, but here in the new role of "Coach" to me. She swam competitively in college and teaches swim lessons, and she has the shoulders to prove it. I pushed off the wall, and after one lap down the pool and back, she noted: "Dano, you don't finish your stroke." *What?* For the past two years, apparently I had taken my arm out of the water to begin the next stroke before it ever made it to the end of the first. No wonder why keeping a "high elbow" seemed so easy - I never straightened it out!

From the deck, she could see it in seconds - but how was I to know? I had read books, watched videos, and practiced drills. From these I could measure increases in my own speed and endurance, and really feel the improvements I was making. But from the outside, a coach could see it entirely differently. Focusing my mind, I made an adjustment and all of a sudden could feel what she was talking about, and although my muscle memory kept pulling my habits back like a tight rubber band, I began breaking through to a new way of moving. The result of fixing a mechanical glitch, to get more out of each swim stroke without putting in any more effort, was nothing short of instant free speed.

Jogging my memory, I faintly recall another afternoon, at my favorite local triathlon shop back when I first began running and sought out a pair of running shoes. They put me on their treadmill and recorded my running, then played it back in slow-motion. The video showed clearly what I would never see from my vantage point: as each foot struck the ground, the ankle rolled inward as it absorbed my weight - a motion known as overpronation. It's a natural motion for humans, but it can have ramifications for the knees and hips over many miles. They brought out shoes that help stabilize this motion, and I could run more comfortably than ever. Not surprisingly, addressing a stability issue at my foot helped make my shins, knees, and hips all feel better when I ran: these other joints were able to achieve better alignment from the ground up.

Some people try to get into running, feel sore, and give up, never knowing what went wrong. As someone who loves the sport and wants it to be accessible, I feel sad when someone wants to try it but just doesn't have trusted partners to help them with the essential tips. It's not intuitive that the structure of one's shoe can result in sensations way up at the hip - especially to someone just getting started. Some people make their purchases based on ads, shoe color, or fads, and never realize the role certain shoes actually play in supporting their endeavor. The outside view of my footstrike clarified my own body mechanics in a way that I couldn't see, and truly made running possible for me. And so much more comfortable.

I'm amazed with the body's complexities and interconnections, and often surprised at the cause and effect pairings. Discovering the complicated makeup and power of my own mind and body has been one of the most exciting parts of this journey. I make discoveries by practicing swimming, biking, and running, and also by reading and attending clinics and listening to others. It takes perspective to know that everything shared by someone else must be translated into the practices that work best for me, but I feel grateful that others are generous enough to share their expertise because they care.

Set another scene on a hot June day, me in my racing outfit, dripping with sweat and slowly walking off the intensity of a sprint-distance triathlon. After my heart rate came down and I replenished with water and electrolytes (and lots of cookies), I spotted a special "free massage" tent set up near the finish area. I was impressed that although the massage therapist and I had never met before, she was able to offer immediate relief to my tired body that I didn't know was available.

I wanted to learn more - and also wanted to give her some remuneration for her efforts on race day - so I scheduled a full hour-long visit. Plus, the quiet peace of her office was a place more conducive to deeper healing than the lively finish line at a race. I tried to think about nothing but breathing, relaxing, sinking into the table, and paying attention to what she was doing.

As she worked deep into my muscles, I realized that in that hour, she knew more about me than I did. Through her expertise she knew where to look for knots and bumps and misery that I couldn't identify, even though these were all within my own body, and had been for some time. Out of respect for her skills and desire to receive the most benefit I could from them, I allowed myself to surrender to her art form, and in doing so was able to be transformed.

Her expertise may have discovered the physical manifestations of my discomfort, but it was something more like compassion - the outside observer's willingness not just to evaluate but to connect and heal - that made all the difference in helping me. It tapped into the human innate need for touch, for connecting to other beings, and I felt a certain oneness with her and the world during the hour. Freeing a person's frozen muscles is more than a physical task, it comes with the joy of freeing them from restrictions holding them back from the full expressions of their lives. I floated away from the session feeling deeply grateful, and greatly liberated.

The implications reach beyond what is apparent: each of us is an outside observer of many others, and has the opportunity to share our specializations for everyone's benefit. Teachers and mentors have expertise to share with students; farmers have food to share with communities; wealthy people have resources to share with poor... What might you want to offer?

BECOMING A LEADER

It's just after 5:00 a.m., and with a cup of hot tea beside me, my typing joins the morning bird-songs. How did I get here? Sometimes I wonder: who would want to read about my experience anyway? If everyone is motivated by something different, how could my message resonate with anyone else? For that matter, what do I have to accomplish before I can consider myself a "writer?" But I also notice the stack of books and magazines and DVD's that have guided me and suggested to me all sorts of interesting new ways to go about my life. Perhaps there is more commonality than I thought, and perhaps my own words will find their way into the canon of motivation, whether to many or only a few. Whether you pick them up and read them is up to you; all I can do is write them down, and be willing to share.

Among my own mantras are *ride your own ride, race your own race*. All you can do is stick to what you believe in and have prepared for, and the "results" will do what they will. I have taken on my racing challenges on my terms. I went about my training, as I had set it up - trying to keep it consistent and harmonious with my overall life priorities. Over time, my consistent practice of swimming, biking, running, and otherwise training gave way to a lifestyle. What could simply be called "training" still does remain preparation for certain races, but serves an intrinsic purpose in itself. Training *is* the goal. Anymore, the effects that training has on me *are* the reason for doing it; racing at the end of a training cycle is just a celebration of the prior period. This is the fascinating phenomenon of becoming the goals I set out to achieve.

The very first time I took my new racing bike out for a spin, I was enthralled by how it fit perfectly, operated smoothly, and flew unstoppably down the pavement. It was like driving a race car after years in a sedan. Although ultimately it is the rider's muscles that make the bike move fast - *there's no substitute for the engine* - I discovered that the bike in fact did make *me* faster. On that first ride down the bike path, I passed other riders just like I had done over the years. I said hello, but I noticed them looking at the bike, and even turning their heads as I went by. I didn't have much life experience with others turning to look at me, and I was surprised. I wasn't trying to show off, but all of a sudden, people were looking at me differently. Could this be what it meant to be *hot*?

In that moment I knew I had a new and important obligation: If I'm going to ride around on this hot bike, I must be the operator who deserves it. I am accountable to myself - and to this bicycle, and will respect its grandeur with the level of training it demands. Buying the bike almost immediately put to rest a long list of potential worries, because I found my bike training suddenly moving to a higher level, a new level of confidence. When I'm on this bike, I am a champion! Knowing what it's like to feel like a champion, even if at first just on a bike, slowly starts to permeate other layers of life. Indeed it took me far - through 112 miles toward the title of "Ironman finisher," which I also carry every day. With the accomplishments come accountability: other people are watching.

As a participant in Team In Training, I was nurtured from the beginning by caring leaders. It was a far different experience from the alienation of middle-school team sports.

Team In Training gave me the framework in which to discover my own abilities, and with time, I became more experienced and more confident. Fortunately, I was also given the opportunity to volunteer as a leader when subsequent seasons brought new participants to the program. Though I do like the calm of quietly moving across the countryside alone, I find a much deeper relationship with the sport by helping introduce others to it, sharing energy and motivation. I can act as a catalyst for other people's good work.

I get a fantastic feeling watching teammates' successes: a first 10-mile run, a first 20-mile run, a first thousand dollars raised, another doubt vanquished by accomplishment. As time and seasons went on, I gained more experience, and became more comfortable sharing it with new members of the team. Some noticed that I had answers to basic questions... then intermediate questions. Nothing specific happened to define the beginning point of "becoming a leader," it just unfolded as a matter of course. I don't think I can pinpoint an event that began this transformation, which is perhaps why looking back on my life and realizing that I've evolved into someone so different can feel so surreal.

As a leader, faith in someone else pays double-dividends: watching that person feel the satisfaction of their success, I feel the same in myself. Their success doesn't take anything away from me; a personal "win" for them is far from any kind of loss for me. On the first day of a new season, I excitedly greet the new sign-ups, and see the questioning look on their faces that suggests *"who is this wacky guy and what on earth have I gotten myself into?"* I see right through the doubt to their ear-to-ear smile at the finish line; I believe in people and their potential. I know that many people - particularly ones who join a charity team - are motivated for many reasons, but apprehensive for many more. I can show them that walking and running are so much more than they might have guessed, and the outcome will extend far beyond physical "fitness." Some struggle to comprehend being referred to as an "athlete" for the first time - just as I still contemplate what it means to be a "coach."

One of the challenges I've experienced in coaching has been learning to listen. I developed into the role by consistently upholding what I believed to work well for myself - only to realize that to be a positive and productive part of someone else's goals, I have to step back and appreciate that their goals may be entirely different than mine. While I might offer guidance on how to achieve them, it's not my place to pigeonhole someone by judging their goals. I try to keep quiet, because others' experiences can differ so vastly from mine, and result in different approaches. When I listen, I've sometimes been surprised to hear my own words - coming from the newer leaders, just as they were passed down from my coach to me - in slightly new versions, propagating the DNA of the program, with a touch of evolution mixed in. People need the chance to grow, but need the space to do it on their own terms, and it's only by listening that I'll discover where I can be a helpful contributor.

When I remember what has unfolded on my way to becoming a leader, I can pipe down with the confidence that I don't have anything to prove. The best way I can lead is the same way I came to become a leader in the first place - by doing what I like to do, in the best way I believe I can. By example, of both fitness and principles. Just as my new race bike made me accountable to my ride, my title of "coach" asks me to always be upstanding. People may begin following my training plans or doing what I suggest, but only as long as these instructions remain relevant to their abilities and goals. I am learning to find the sweet spot where my own successes are relevant and motivating to others, without boasting.

The real motivators, the ones that work, are the ones that come from within. The ones that are founded on something understandable, something related enough to existing values that they can take on real meaning. As such, I recognize that what motivates me isn't necessarily the same thing that motivates other people... sometimes. A whole new level of satisfaction and personal pride comes from seeing potential in other people right from the beginning, which they cannot see, and watching it blossom into achievement over the course of the season. As a coach, I *am* the benevolent observer. The best satisfaction is in saying "see, I told you so" - to myself, even though I have often wanted to say it out loud. The accomplishment will speak for itself, and say it for me.

Obviously I can never go back to my own "firsts," but as a coach, I can share the unbridled, dumbfounded, overwhelming triumph with each athlete whose season culminates at a particular finish line. In my own training sessions and races, I continue to seek the first-timers' excitement. Perhaps this is why, in spite of becoming a much stronger athlete, I have enjoyed remaining a part of beginner-friendly teams, rather than seek out only the "fastest" ones. Even while experience challenges me to pursue tougher races, higher standings, and greater speed, I still hang on to my original priorities of doing it all for joy - along with my health, a greater mission, and friend-making. The more I'm able to remain as excited as I was at the beginning, the more I'm able to contribute to the sport and those trying it out around me.

I believe that the human body is a complicated and brilliant machine that can adapt and thrive in more situations than many people give it credit for, and I believe that not attempting to actualize this miracle is one of the saddest tragedies of modern American sedentary life. I'm grateful for all of the organizations and individuals who put efforts into encouraging people to get moving and discover more inside themselves than they knew. When ordinary people take the leap of faith to begin this journey, I watch them discover whole new elements of life they had not seen before: greater courage, deeper faith, broader horizons in a bigger world. Not just better health but fuller well-being. Needless to say, I am excited for each season ahead.

RACE REPORT:
SAN DIEGO MARATHON

Just when I think it doesn't get any better - it does. Again and again, the marathon takes me to higher mountaintops and shows me the purest beauties of life and the human spirit. People coming together and encouraging without boundaries, all while pushing themselves beyond physical limits they thought possible. When I went to San Diego in 2011, I wasn't just going for the marathon, I was going as a coach. I had made it: coaching in the big game.

Not only did the marathon draw some 30,000 runners, over 3,000 of them were Team In Training participants from all 57 chapters across the US and Canada, who raised over 9 million dollars to fight cancer. That's serious stuff. That says to anyone going through treatment or grieving a loss "we are with you, in full force." I realized that I had an important role - I was both leading the group, and curating the experience.

On Friday morning before the race, I drove from Madison to Milwaukee to catch our plane. I offered a ride to one of my runners, and the car ride flew by as we recalled stories from the season; she considered with incredulity how the weekend of her first marathon had finally arrived. At the airport, we met up with the runners from Milwaukee. Friday morning, this group of groggy acquaintances exchanged brief, pleasant introductions during breaks from texting friends and wrapping up other tasks from the week; by Friday evening we moved as a group, sharing personal stories, and fully engulfed in our Californian vacation. What a blessing to let go of the ordinary for a weekend and dive headlong into an experience.

I helped keep an eye on everyone through the lens of their upcoming race - pointing out drinking fountains, suggesting easy activities, avoiding long hours on our feet. We first visited the race expo to pick up our packets, and I took photos as teammates received their first-ever marathon number bibs. When one was reluctant to buy a really nice-looking race jacket, I reminded her that she will only have one "first marathon." I'm glad I helped give her permission to splurge a bit, because she loves the jacket and wears it all the time. Not surprisingly, when I came across a snazzy "Coach" jacket, I bought it!

We had dinner together in San Diego's gas lamp district and got to know each other. One of the most important things Team In Training teaches us is that you just never know: you never know what kinds of life situations teammates have left at home for the respite of event weekend. You never know what kind of connection they have to the cause or how dangerously close they've been to cancer. The night before the race, Team In Training holds an inspiration dinner, during which we honor all the survivors. When they stand up, it's always a surprise to see who's been through it, but has never even mentioned it. Imagine what life would be like if we treated everyone like we just discovered they were facing insurmountable odds. Try it today.

Saturday morning, as the runners slept in one last time before race day, I attended a staff meeting. Literally hundreds gathered to prepare; I loved it. There I was: getting the inside scoop on all the details for the San Diego Marathon. I was not just on the backstage tour, I was getting my assignments for the show, I was playing my part in a well-orchestrated symphony designed to motivate and move. I got my first "coach" number bib - but no chip. Coaches are allowed on the course, and we do a lot of running, but we don't do it for ourselves, we do it for the participants. I like to think of it in terms of the old race rule: "No chip, no time"... *no problem!* I did have my own secret personal goal of running my first 50-k over the course of the day, which I would track using my GPS watch, but that goal was secondary to the task of helping each and every runner keep moving forward.

My teammates decided that our day-before-the-race activity would be a trip to the beach, since we were so close to the Pacific. Plus, the adventure would include a good deal of time riding public transit, as a fine way to see a slice of the city, but remain seated, per coach's advice. Jess stepped up to the plate with her excellent trip-planning and -guiding skills, and led us to the water, where she dipped her hand in the Pacific for the first time. I kicked back and enjoyed the ride, casually watching over the group and periodically redirecting them toward smarter pre-race decisions, but otherwise trying to stay out of the way of their creating their own experience. A good coach knows when *not* to be the leader. We took plenty of photos at the beach before eating a healthy, easy-to-digest lunch, then heading back for our inspiration party and bed time. Race day was upon us.

With a start time of 6:15 a.m., we met in the hotel lobby at 3:45 a.m. to catch our bus. Though I had my things laid out and my alarm set for 3:20, at 2:55 my eyes opened and I was wide awake. I think you can determine commitment to a race by how excited you are when you wake up early. I slathered on sunscreen, suited up, packed a bag of everything I thought a coach ought to have on the course, and headed down. *This is it.*

In the wee hours of the morning, when the team was a combination of groggy, nervous, and excited, I was there to lead them. Hopefully they were a little less anxious knowing that I had their back: I ensured that each one had a timing chip, number bib, sunscreen, and body glide. I brought sports drinks and energy gels; I took photos the whole way to help them later rebuild the stories otherwise forgotten in the race-morning haze. I helped them put on plastic bags on the way to the starting line so they didn't shiver away their energy stores, and pointed them toward port-a-potties with the shortest lines.

I was fortunate to have been assigned coaching duty between miles 22 - 26.2, so that I would have time in the early morning to actually start the race with my team, before moving to the other end of the course. The faster runners on our team voluntarily moved back so that we could all toe the line together, and we were early enough to claim a spot right at the front of the starting corral. The race began and each corral moved slowly forward, until finally only a little yellow string separated us from the marathon. The open road was before us, our worries were behind us, and all our training was inside us. I shouted my final piece of advice: "THIS IS NOT A DRILL!" The horn blew and the moment arrived that we had all been waiting for.

Once I reached mile 1 of the marathon with my team, it was time to head for my coaching assignment: time to short cut over to mile 22. I leapt off an overpass and suddenly was at the mile 10 mark down below. I ran along (and even saw the Kenyans come by in the lead) for about 5 miles, making a couple stops to check the map and scramble up embankments or across medians and whatnot, to traverse the course in the quickest way. Although I wasn't going to get a medal, it was a thrilling pursuit of the finish line, different from "usual" marathon-running. My assignment was one of the toughest parts of the race: the island. At mile 22, runners see the finish line in front of them, but must make a turn and travel around a 3-mile island, devoid of any trees or even features. And there I waited in the shade of a UPS truck until the first purple shirt arrived.

He came up with another coach, and as I joined them the other coach quickly briefed me that this runner was seeking to qualify for Boston and holding firm to a mid-7-minute-per-mile pace. The runner himself barely spoke - he was right at the breaking point. So I said a few words of encouragement, and quietly ticked along with him for nearly two miles at his perfect pace, minding the task at hand, frequently checking my watch to honor his goal. Once he got to the next water station and the next coach, my day had truly begun: I turned back and ran *upstream*, alongside the course, cheering on the runners until the next purple shirt arrived. Soon enough, a tall, fit and jovial fellow came cruising along and I joined him. I asked how many marathons he had run and he replied casually "oh, I don't know, a bunch... but this is my first one back since treatment." He survived cancer and also qualified for Boston; what stands between you and *your* goals?

As another man approached, he saw me and beckoned me over to run with him; he was struggling to hold on to his goal pace. I asked about his honored patient-hero, and suddenly his marathon-struggle seemed to be alleviated as his perspective changed. I liked being recognized as someone who could help. As runners came through, I drifted farther and farther downstream, until I eventually stuck with one runner all the way to the finish line. It's the best thing a coach can do: jump in alongside someone and support them in the toughest parts of their journey. I said to her, "I'll turn back now, or if you'd like I'll stick with you." "Could you stay with me a little longer?" "Yes, I will stay with you all the way to the end." Yes, that is indeed what it's all about.

Soon enough, the runners from Wisconsin came by, one by one. I had hoped to run with each of them around the whole island, because it was so tough - and they each recounted later thinking "where's Dano?!" I know, I know - I ran as fast as I could to get back up the course, but I kept getting so excited when I saw a runner who seemed to need my help, I kept being swept downstream and mostly stayed between miles 25 and 26. They came by in various states of physical well-being, but all of them were positive and excited about the finish. I was so moved as I sent them into the finish chute. I can only have my own first marathon once, but on that day I went to the finish 13 times, and, like them, was emotional every time. I could think of nothing I would rather have been doing than bringing home these runners all day long.

All told, I exceeded my own distance goal by running 34 miles in my 8-hour-10-minute day on the course. Each time I went to the end, I thought: "give me more!" I overheard some spectators say "there he goes again!" I had a contagious and ravenous high - I couldn't get enough of it. It didn't matter that I didn't cross the finish line, but that the people I was coaching did. When I stopped each time at the entrance of the finish chute, I could see their arms rise in elation as they ran away from me, toward the cameras and cheering fans and medals. So much hard work, faith, patience, courage, and perseverance goes into finishing a marathon. The reward is a feeling of satisfaction so overwhelming that you feel indestructible, and earn a title of "marathon finisher" that cannot ever be taken away.

The day concluded as the final Team In Training participant walked down that final stretch. As she progressed along the course, each coach and staff member fell in line with her - so that as she approached 26.2 miles, she wasn't last and she sure wasn't alone: 300 of us all joined her across the finish line. In our camp, nobody ever gets left behind.

Sometimes I tell non-runner friends and colleagues about the races I go to, and they ask if I won, or who won the race. I just have to smile and chuckle, because I know what it means to put a mission before a finish line, or even before the race itself. I've been to a pre-race dinner in the biggest convention hall in San Diego that could only hold half of my charity group. I've felt the burning pain in my legs and the burning doubt in my mind as the finish line lingered far in front of me, and I've leant my shoulder to others feeling the same way. I've run alongside men and women who had a disease once called "100 percent fatal," on their way to finishing the greatest challenge in running. I'll tell you who the winner is in this race: the one wearing a purple shirt.

TAKING IT OUT INTO THE WORLD

The thrill of victory doesn't fade overnight. Long after the race ends, the crowds have gone home, and the rest of life returns, you're still a finisher. It's been said "there will be days you don't know whether you can run a marathon, and a lifetime of knowing that you have." Indeed. That medal has earned its prominent position on the wall forever. Even if it should be lost, along with all the internet's ostensibly permanent finisher-databases, the victory still remains. Many things come and go in this life, but these major accomplishments, once completed, cannot be undone. And they leave a permanent mark that can be used for an even greater benefit.

On Tuesday morning after the San Diego marathon, I re-entered my ordinary daily life at work. Only, I hadn't yet cut my hair, which I had dyed bright green for the race. A little part of my mind wanted to be concerned that I would be made fun of for standing out, and I certainly knew that I'd hear a lot of remarks, but another part told me it didn't matter. In fact, I thought it looked sharp with a white shirt and silver tie. Even if I didn't think it would be relevant to anyone else, I believed firmly that what I had done was good and true. I understood that the abstract concept of raising money in parallel with a race, for the sake of helping others, does not end at the finish line of the race; I think the recipients of Team In Training's efforts would appreciate that.

As it turned out, most of my coworkers' remarks were positive, and our conversations became opportunities to talk about my race as a charity athlete. Many people learned something fundamental about me they hadn't known. Many heard for the first time that some people do races to help others. In my workplace there aren't a lot of people who have attempted an endurance event, and others who don't even know what that means. But there's something about it that gets them excited when I start to talk about it. Maybe they're picking up on my excitement.

The best reaction seems to come when I mention the amount of money Team In Training raises at an event: then it seems to click for them why a coach might go over the top with something like green hair to show his commitment to his athletes. I'm proud of what my team has accomplished and I'm glad to talk about it. I'm eager to invite more people to join us. I'm comfortable talking about our mission and the fundraising that supports it, because I believe in it. Even if I may appear a little goofy at first, it's worth standing out.

It may have started with the endeavor of fundraising. When I first joined the program and committed to raising money along with training, I reached out to friends, neighbors, coworkers, and family members. I told them about the program, and asked them for contributions. As replies came back, I was surprised by the huge amount of support I received, often from those I least expected. Along with several of the replies were notes about close encounters with cancers - notes about a mix of loss, uncertainty, and remission. Asking family and friends at first felt a little awkward; reaching further required more of a leap of faith.

I really left my comfort zone when I decided to knock on every door on my street and ask for donations from neighbors. I started with "Hi, I'm Dan Tyler from number 65. You're going to see me out here running in the snow over the next few months, and I'd like to tell you why." I think it was the "running in the snow" bit that got most people's attention and helped them warm up to me as a neighbor and not some kind of salesman. I had met a few of my neighbors before, but certainly not to this extent. I personally don't care for this sort of cold call, but just kept pushing myself to make all the visits.

I learned that one neighbor had lost nearly all her family to cancers; another sat on the front porch with me for half an hour talking about the history of the neighborhood. One gave me some money after hearing what his wife had already given me and grumbling his opinion that it was too stingy. One told me about her experiences working with Leukemia patients at the hospital. When I reached the end of the street, I was invited to a kitchen table to share annual bicycling goals. Unexpectedly, my fundraising effort pushed me to connect in a deeper way with humanity. When I walk down my street today, I wave and call these people by name, and I feel home.

It was a good exercise in setting judgment and fear aside, because you just never know. You never know who will give and who won't; you never know someone's circumstances for being able to give or not; you never know who might personally be the very cause you are working for. You learn to never say "no" *for* anyone, but to always ask compassionately. From the safety of the team's framework, I pushed myself to reach out to the greater humanity - and realized that "they" are not really all that separate from "us."

Similarly, with the completion of each race - after invariably feeling doubts and challenges during it - I gain a little more confidence in myself. From within the controlled, small, discrete, and safe environment of a race, I can nudge my own boundaries and discover my own strength, in spite of temporary discomfort. With opportunities to be a leader within my Team, and help guide someone else toward their own successes, I see broader implications; it's not just about the races. It's about a kind of fitness or strength that goes much further, permeating daily relationships and interactions. It's about a kind of resolve that comes with knowing that conditions always change, mountaintops must come with valleys, and people need one another's support on the journey. I mean, it *could* just be all about the races, but really, what good would that do?

In my race setting, a simple pin reading "26.2" symbolizes all the hard work that goes into a season with the Team. But it generally only holds meaning to those who understand it. As soon as I head home, my accomplishments at the race which were celebrated by people who knew what they meant become my own responsibility to hold in my own heart as reminders of how I should behave. The fans along the marathon course that made the biggest impressions on me were those who cheered for complete strangers like they were family. I think the people who make the biggest impressions on the world are those who don't need a marathon to treat others like that.

When the street is closed and I'm in uniform moving down the road inside the barricades, my life has a special purpose and meaning - I have a special right of way. But that changes on Monday morning, when I take the sidewalk to work and have to find my own way. I wonder if this is a little slice of what a soldier - a hero decorated in a special context - must face as she puts on her plain clothes and tries to find meaning in the anonymous crowd that doesn't see her accomplishments. Does this begin to describe the long blank page upon which a cancer patient must begin to write after the last "I'm in remission!" party guest leaves? We rally around those who are struggling, but how are we doing in the day-to-day? I don't pretend to believe that even my most grueling race compares to these challenges, but I have learned that people carry around all kinds of hidden accomplishments, and hidden baggage.

Consider your immediate attitude change when you discover that someone is dealing with a very challenging problem. Imagine what life would be like if you treated everyone you met with the same intentional compassion as in that moment of realization. The world is filled with people facing tough situations like illness, hardship, or pain. I talk about Team In Training and its mission often - in buses and airplanes and meeting rooms. If green hair gets the conversation going, so much the better. Time and time again, in reply come personal stories of the way cancer has touched the people whose lives cross paths with mine. During a job interview an HR manager began to cry; on a flight across the country a seatmate explained losing her mother just the week before.

Imagine if, in every interaction with a friend or stranger alike, each person treated every other as if they were on a short break from sitting with a sick friend or relative - what kind of peace would the world learn to embrace? Humanity needs that from itself. Immersing myself in this charity training program has not just taught me how to swim, bike, and run a long way, it's taught me a great lesson: you just never know. It's taught me that these truths discovered within the race microcosm can and should be nurtured and generalized, translated into the tenets of a healthy, compassionate life.

VERY HARD THINGS

We all have to face very hard situations in our lives. They're going to erupt after long periods of smoldering, or explode out of nowhere. And they're not going to stop, either - the spacing will just change. Some are going to be much harder than others. In my experience - I'm sure much like many others' - I've been frustrated when unexpected challenges come up and I stammer or stumble, but I've found ways to prepare. I think we are drawn to super-hard tests - to races like the marathon - in order to practice.

The races themselves are a unique kind of life-training: they let us practice intense pain and significant doubt within a generally positive experience. We can intentionally create a situation that is very hard, and gain experience overcoming it within the relative safety of its specificity. In doing so, in spite of the doubts that invariably accompany it, we come to realize that if we jump in and persevere, we can make it through more than we think.

Out on the road, as the long miles pass under foot or wheel, there's plenty of time for contemplation. There's time to learn to be OK with yourself - just you, moving along. It can be rich with sights of nature's bounty otherwise unnoticed, or rich with inward vision through a meditative eye. As we came to the top of a long climb one Sunday morning, a friend and I gazed over the green land all around us, and I said "I'm glad we skipped church this morning;" he replied, "I *am* in church."

When I spend time in training on my own, I have the opportunity to get to know myself, to consider who I am and what I'm doing; where I want to go, and what greater universal connections might be taking me there. It's healthy introspective time away from everything else in life. I know many parents who yearn for this reprieve, not because they do not love their children or desire to be distant from them, but because the solo time gives them the space to rejuvenate and become a better person and parent. Away from others, pursuing a very personal goal, we are able to feel valid not based on another's judgment or approval, but on our own terms.

I distinctly remember the Friday morning I left my house early and rode a long bike ride I had ridden several times before - but always previously with friends. This time, I set out on my own, and somewhere in the middle of an 80-mile ride from Wisconsin to Illinois, surrounded by silence and corn fields, I realized that I was truly a long way from home, and all alone. I felt only a moment of uneasiness with the solitude before turning my attention to my capacity for completing such a feat on my own. I felt well-prepared with food, water, map, and tire-changing equipment. Although no one was there to see me, or race against me, I was strong.

Conditions will change, of this I am sure. No matter how well-prepared or experienced a person is, surprises will occur on race day that are different than those he or she prepared for. Even with the simple passage of time, things must necessarily be different from moment to moment. The pavement we run and ride upon heaves and cracks under rain and sunshine and snowplows, the lakes in which we swim freeze and thaw and host animals and bacteria that come and go in a delicate ecological balance from one millisecond to the next. Lives, large and small, come and go around us as our own adapts and changes - and I find myself standing at another starting line a completely different person than I was in preparation for the very same moment. Sometimes it's scary, because it means that I will not know all the answers, and I will not be able to specifically prepare for everything.

Conditions will change, of this I am sure - and in this dynamic is also liberation. Because not only will certain comforts eventually end, but so will whatever frustration or fear may be pulling me down in a moment. During a long hill climb, I can lean on the knowledge that if I just deal with the discomfort for a while, it too will end - usually with a view. In the lake, during a crowded, splashy swim, I remind myself that the sensation of panic rushing through my body is a natural physiological reaction, evolved to keep me from being eaten by a saber-toothed tiger. I sight to the next buoy and suggest that I turn my attention toward the complexities of my form and breath - *just go to the next buoy and future-me will take it from there*. The human brain itself responds to conditioning, a remarkable ability accessible through consistent training. Overwhelming fears, whether real or completely fabricated, will pass if they are let go.

If my goal in a race is to finish before a competitor, I'm still limited to doing my own best on race day. The same will hold true for the other, and our respective abilities will change from day to day. No two competitions will ever be alike, from who shows up to what the weather brings. The best that I will have to offer on race day is largely my decision, based on how willing I am to make the best of the day, and how much I am willing to endure. It will be based to an even larger degree on how I've trained throughout the season: regardless of the standings, I have control of my own commitment to training and racing. I enjoy the democracy of sharing the same course and conditions. I appreciate the judiciousness of earning the results that I deserve on the basis of what I put in. Of course, a bit of good luck helps, too.

If the race is something you want, you will decide to continue toward your goal in spite of the changes that inevitably occur. Victory doesn't look exactly like you envisioned it. You might realize that changes aren't as devastating as you thought - or that, in fact, you became stronger because of them. Stronger in a sense much broader than power output by muscles; rather, in the ability to overcome challenging situations. The greatest outcome of training is not so much to become faster, but to become more adaptable. As training yields sharper physical abilities, we realize that we are ready for all kinds of other tests in which we may be called upon to perform. We realize that we have not just become more ready to deal with the issues that come up during a race, but have become more resilient to all nature of challenges that life may deal us.

Which leads to perhaps the most fundamental truth: *you can't pick the weather on race day*. You can practice in all kinds of conditions (or not), but the weather will come down to chance. Or fate, or karma - or whatever you want to call it. In fairness, the conditions will be the same for everyone racing. The forecasts will allow racers to prepare and make general decisions. And after that - it's all about what you make of it; no degree of complaining will make any difference, besides perhaps what others think of you for having to listen to it. Race-day weather may be the greatest indicator of the athlete ready to make excuses and place asterisks in his diaries versus the athlete ready to look deep inside for strength. For me, a rainy day may mean slower turns on the bike or different running shoes, but no less fun in the race, and certainly no less of a challenge. *Did you sign up because you wanted it to be easy?*

As a matter of fact, you can't pick the weather any day: it's best to bring your own. The most important element of preparing - in the broadest sense - is becoming adaptable. Retaining what's important to me at the heart of the things I do, in spite of the parts that don't look like what I expected. Though I do love a calm, mild day, I welcome rain and wind as a chance to shine. I don't call weather "awful" just like I don't gripe over terrain: these are part of the physical challenge, the tests of the race. It's in these situations that I notice myself adjusting my race-day plan to accommodate the challenges as best I can, but notice many others struggling miserably. Because my attitude does not come from the weather, but does contribute to my output, I thrive in adverse conditions.

Mental and physical, the top priority of my training is to make myself less susceptible to exterior conditions; to accept the race environment for what it is, and do the best I can with it. Practicing intentionally making the environment more uncomfortable trains the mind to be resilient amidst the uncertainties of the race day environment, and leaves more space for joy and thanksgiving. It's become a habit that has extended beyond the bounds of the race course: I feel indestructible. No, not all the time - but more frequently than before. I know that I can endure very hard things, and I can keep going in spite of significant challenges. I know that there are certain things that I can control or plan for, and others that I must take as they come. I've gained confidence and courage for dealing with "regular" life as a result of overcoming the challenges of training and racing.

Everyone has to deal with very hard situations in life, in one form or another. Training and racing - especially to my very best - take me out to the edge of where I think I can hang on, and invite me to stay there, solely on the strength of my own will. When life's challenges pile up and I feel ready to collapse, I have a special kind of faith that I discovered at mile twenty-something, or at some physical threshold - something inside that just kept me moving forward. Very hard situations will keep coming at us, and sometimes they'll feel endless underfoot, but the races teach us to believe in ourselves, and just keep putting one foot in front of the other.

WHY WAIT?

When I graduated from college with my engineering degree, I went to work for a very large, well-respected construction firm. Their repertoire included impressive multi-billion-dollar construction projects that very few companies were able to tackle; they had offices all around the country; their stock consistently returned double-digit dividends. Frankly, I loved it. In the first year, I worked from headquarters, saw a lot of projects, and had the opportunity to travel to many job sites around the country. When training ended, I moved to an office near New York and worked about 50 hours a week.

Then one day, the boss called me into his office, said he was sending me to a project in Tampa, and off I went to look for a new home, again. By the time I was one year into a three-year construction project, I worked twelve hours a day, six days a week... sometimes only eight on Saturdays. Little bits of leisure squeezed in between working, commuting, preparing food for the next work day, and sleeping - which seemed to keep slipping down on the priority list in spite of the year-long headache that developed.

Every once in a while, I'd email friends from past projects. Some of them continued their tenure at the company in spite of the moves and the hours, while others bailed out. I still remember the chill I felt when I read one friend's response: he had been in a serious car crash, and foggily recalled a bystander pulling him out of his burning, rolled-over SUV. At that moment, he said, it was clear to him that it was time for a change; time to start focusing on things that were really important to him. These kinds of stories have become an essential part of the canon in busy American life: in speeches, sermons, and seminars. When we hear them, don't we invariably respect those people for making their decisions? Don't we often think, "Wow, if only I could do that" about our own over-busy lives?

About the same time, I got a call one evening from an old friend: he had bad news. He was one of those few old friends who went way back - back to the beginning of high school - and who had faithfully insisted on retaining these friendships through high school, college, first jobs, cross-country moves, and all sorts of different directions. One of our old friends was sick, we discovered, with a cancer that had already progressed to an advanced stage by the time the pain caused her to visit the doctor. We barely got to talk about it - by the time she was diagnosed, it was out of control and inoperable; we had a couple of phone conversations, though I hardly knew how to react or what to say.

Her widely-spread tumors and limited insurance left her with few treatment options besides chemotherapy, that intentionally-poisoning cocktail which doctors hope will kill the cancer before it kills the patient. She was in bed at our old stomping grounds in Ohio, and I felt like I had to stay at work in Florida. By the time I made it home for Thanksgiving, she wasn't able to talk anymore, but I still held her hand and offered her some words of my own. The next afternoon, I sat at her side talking lightly with her single mom and one other friend, while quietly and without regalia she took her last breath.

I guess by pressing "publish," this is my big reveal. I seldom bring it up, even with my closest friends or teammates.

In my Team In Training setting, many people choose to tell their stories of how cancer has affected their lives, and these stories are moving and motivating. I'm glad they do - they call charity athletes to action, with impressive results. I laugh with some of my friends who are survivors of cancer that it's so much easier for them to raise money! Others prefer not to say: one teammate had wanted to complete her first half-marathon to honor her recently-diagnosed mother, but the mom didn't want to be "outed" as having cancer - she didn't want to be known as someone sick.

I keep my story quiet because I don't feel that I deserve special consideration because my best friend died from cancer. I want to be recognized for my hard work, generosity, and caring. If someone listens to what I say as a coach, I want it to be because I have said something worthwhile. If someone respects me for volunteering with a charity organization, I want it to be because I have chosen to volunteer and have made a meaningful contribution through my own effort, not because life handed me an unfortunate situation. And I so desperately want people to care for each other without regard for their circumstances.

Over the four-year course of compiling this memoir, one situation after another arose and took its place on the front page of the newspaper. The earthquake shook Haiti and there was an outpouring of monetary and volunteer support. It was hip and helpful to text support, hold concerts, send supplies, and volunteer time. But meanwhile and heroically, other volunteers were there working all along - living there, immersed in the culture - some of whom even died in the earthquake alongside Haitian people. They didn't need an earthquake to identify a need, and were willing to take a chance and quietly offer what the world needed from them. Later, the world watched as 33 men were removed from a mine in Chile; across borders and languages and sides of wars past, human beings hoped that other human beings' story would have a happy ending. Afterward, a handful of people made the leap to make a change in their own lives, and millions of others slid back into the momentum of their status quo.

In a way, I wish I could report some momentous epiphany that realigned my priorities; I even think it would sell more books. But I've come to realize that I don't have to wait for my own near-death experience to make important changes in my life. I haven't had to overcome anything too terrible, I have just had to stand up for what I wanted, and have the courage to initiate changes in directions I didn't exactly know, but that I knew were right.

Why wait? What's between you and your life as it is today, and the life that you want to be living? Were you planning to wait for some world-shaking tragedy or distinct epiphany before giving your priorities a good going-over? Because you might just not make it through alive, so you'll get a lot farther by just standing up and going for it now, while you can.

One of my teammates once reflected on the best gift: the gift of time. I remember the day we met, when she came to an informational meeting, curious about riding a 100-mile century bike ride, but reluctant to commit because of her cancer. I remember feeling shocked in that moment, and proud for being part of a group that raised money to fund research to create drugs to allow her to consider it at all. Not only did she complete the ride, she went on to run a half-marathon the next summer, with a few pointers from Coach Dano. At the team's final meeting before the race, this thin, fit, spritely, smiling woman reflected on those fifteen months of her life. Since her diagnosis, she was able to spend 15 months with her young children and her new friends on the Team. She was unsure of what would happen next, but remained focused on the good fortune to have had "extra" time, filled with rich experiences. I thought of how she had accomplished more in 15 months than many people hope to accomplish in a lifetime - because she refused to give up. Where would you focus your energy if you were given an extra fifteen months to live?

***

It's natural that endurance sports and charity teams go hand in hand. So many of the trials that the long races present can be compared to a charity's mission of helping those dealing with great challenges of their own: endurance and perseverance, making space to help. Cancer patients may be able to muster the strength to remain positive, or be given choices in their treatment options, but to a great extent don't get to pick their health condition. Charity athletes, on the other hand, intentionally take on the pain of the long course, not just in the interest of their own health, but in solidarity for others' health.

Lying in bed the night before a race, and making our way to the starting line, worries about the incessant unknown challenges ahead dance around in our minds. It's important to take on races that are challenging enough that they are unpredictable. They remind us to retain a healthy respect for the race, and remind us of the long and scary journey that our patient-heroes travel.

During the long sessions, in what otherwise might be the loneliest hours, deeper kinds of feelings and relationships become accessible. When the body becomes fatigued from hours of exertion and all of life seems to come down to putting one foot in front of the other, a certain timeless meditation emerges. Here, I find a mysterious confluence of time where I can do some of my most important remembering. I remember friends and family members who have gone before me. I sense soldiers and heroes and legends I have never met, but to whom I owe gratitude. As I move silently down the road alone, the ones who have died become really no different than the ones who live; neither appear physically, but both live in my mind. During our loneliest hours, we can finally get close to our angels, and they propel us.

Everyone has to deal with very hard situations in one way or another, but nobody wants to do it alone. Many people - like me - join a team to try their first race with the support of a group, and come to realize its tremendous power as the season unfolds. We watch out for each other, we celebrate each others' victories and mourn each others' losses that we come to know. The races we pursue come down to individual effort, just like our own lives, so supporting each other ends up not requiring us to necessarily do anything or solve anything for someone else, but simply to show up, be present, and be supportive. Up ahead, there's a glimpse of light from a water station, where cheering fans await an exhausted body with fuel and energy. Being there for someone as they navigate their way through the deepest shadows is *being* love.

Some day, when inevitably I lay dying, I hope family and friends are able to be at my side. But I'm perhaps even more glad that they have been there cheering for me while I'm living. When I consider the highest points in my life, they were the achievements that took the most time and energy, the most dedication and perseverance and usually pain. There in the picture of those fond memories are the people closest to me, time and time again. So too have I shown up in finish photos, my "coach" shirt blurred in the background as a runner triumphantly crosses the finish line.

Life is short. People I've known and who I've read about, who have lived through near-death experiences, describe how they've turned away from overworking and unnecessary stressors to look instead for joy. Voluntarily decreasing my own income in exchange for fewer and more flexible working hours has been one of the best decisions I have ever made, and has allowed me to put the amount of time and effort I want into my own pursuits, including volunteering (and writing). Coaching and racing pay me more than I could have imagined in satisfaction, joy, and life purpose. It gives me a great fullness that swells and wanes through the seasons, culminating each time in race weekend. I suspect it does the same, in one way or another, for my teammates.

Of course, even life itself must come to an end, which is something very complicated to come to terms with. Being a charity athlete can be an emotional roller coaster because it constantly juxtaposes disease, pain, and loss with empowerment, joy, and success - but in these ways it strengthens us for what it teaches about doing all we can for ourselves and for others in the short time that we have together. It shows us that we are stronger than we think, and we are even stronger yet when we support each other. It teaches us how to care, how to endure, and no less than how to love.

PART III
TRI THERAPY

CREDIT FOR CHARACTER

I believe in doing the right thing, and I believe that by doing the right thing, life will somehow be better. "The right thing" is not always evident, and sometimes it's downright opaque. There are often many more "right" choices than just one, and so many factors contribute to what is "right" that sometimes even a long period of soul-searching does not conclude with a definitive direction in which to head off.

To make matters more complicated, what one person calls "right," another might find quite offensive. Each day in the world, interacting with others, we're constantly faced with our choices, in how we live our own lives and how we interact with others. At the bottom line, even if it means trying harder or going out of my way, I try to do what's right. *It's just what you do*.

Through all these decisions and interactions, truly the only thing I can control is my own course of action - including my own reactions. One resource after another advises that being happy, resilient, and healthy begins with a focus inward - managing one's own thoughts and reactions amidst the constant bombardment the world splashes our way. I'm on board, though it's easier said than done. I can get pretty hot pretty fast when I feel injustice: when I feel cheated, cut off, or minimized.

Instances where "bad guys" do nasty things and seem to get away with it make me feel very upset. Maybe their actions impact me indirectly, or maybe hardly at all, but even the notion that injustice exists can be enough to wind me up. I go out of my way to try to do something right - and you want to take advantage of me? Push me? Swoop in and claim for yourself something that I have been working hard for? Take a shortcut but still claim the glory? No way.

I suspect a lot of us hold certain ideals in our lives that are seldom talked about. They are deeply ingrained - things our parents taught us, things we have clung to our whole lives. "The right thing." If I never cheat, no one is ever going to display a document that shows "zero cheats out of 5,000 opportunities!" to some applauding crowd. Perhaps a talented eulogizer might make a remark like "he was a good and honest man," or a compassionate peer may say "he is retiring after years of faithful and dedicated service."

Sometimes we hear a welcome and refreshing "thank you" along the way from someone who notices; sometimes we are recognized because hard work and good work stand out. Even a humble person appreciates the affirmation that recognition brings from time to time - we all need reminders that "good" does in fact prevail. Nobody really knows but us which ideals we've managed to uphold; as a little relief, nor does anyone else know which ideals we've even tried to embody.

On a smaller scale, the races know. The races know whether we've been naughty or nice, and they're not afraid to tell us. No matter what we tell others or how convincingly we respond to "how's training?" there's no hiding the truth from the race itself. The longer the race, the more it speaks up; the closer to first place, all the louder. For a guy who needs to feel that justice does in fact prevail, I cling to these experiences as supporting evidence. Training and racing for me have become a strength-builder for my sense of faith. We bring all sorts of things with us to the starting line - either the start of the season or the start of the race - and getting started takes faith. Keeping going takes faith - and guts - and practice. The finish line gives us proof.

At most races, all it takes to toe the starting line is an on-time application and paid-in-full entry fee. (On another level, sure, it takes courage too - that's another chapter). I guess even a cheater can sneak into the race as a "bandit," without paying the entry fee, but should they make it to the podium, they'd be yanked back down. The course is the great leveler: we all toe the same line, we all follow the same route, we all aim for the same finish line. In this way, the race is very democratic. It's a welcome place bursting with the fullest kind of life, in the pursuit of happiness. Fortunately, liberty also presides as each contestant brings his or her own abilities and goals to the course.

Where I stand in the amateur age-group pack, I race against myself. I sometimes race against the clock to compare this race's outcome to other races' or other years', but mostly toward the very best I have to offer on that day. The more I race, the more I learn about myself, and so the challenge heightens as I inch ever closer to that thin gray line between personal best and complete disaster. If I get faster, perhaps my thin gray line will go right up next to someone else's and we'll be racing each other for first place, but that's not something I currently have much experience with. Rightfully so, because although winning overall is certainly intriguing, I have not dedicated the kind of intensity to my training that I think would merit such a victory.

My very best on race day starts many days before: it starts at some point when I decide to make that race a priority and go get it. In the case of my first iron-distance tri, it started as a dream years before that finally materialized as I signed up, a year prior to the event. Between signing up and toeing the line, the season was mine to capture or squander. Training decisions can represent those "right" decisions - indeed the most meaningful and effective training plan is founded not just on athletic tasks, but on the personal values that brought us to committing to training to begin with. The races aren't just a metaphor for life's challenge to make good choices - they *are* life's choices. Training and racing become part of our value system, both for themselves and for what they represent. The most effective training plan is one you believe in - and so is the one that starts by defining things like "why am I training" or "what role does this play in my life overall?"

Though I am reluctant to say it, for fear that it might sound like boasting, I didn't doubt whether I would make it through those 140.6 miles. I took a lot of time to carefully draw up my plan, address my limiters, celebrate my strengths, and make the training a positive part of my life overall. Barring any catastrophe - and I was careful to manage risks as well - my plan would pay off if I was true to it. I don't mean rigidly following 365 days of workouts, either, because my plan was driven by concepts like patience and flexibility, not just exercise.

When specific workouts or even weekly plans fell through, I regrouped and referred back to the fundamentals behind the plan and continued forward. Plus, the training itself was fun: I met great people, I enjoyed better health, I felt comfort in the schedule. I didn't spend the whole summer looking forward to one day in the fall, but lived each day for what it was, with the confidence that the overarching plan - the values it represented - would lead me to where I wanted to eventually go. This echoes those countless other life situations that ask us to consider our own ideals, and do "what's right."

Eventually, every training period comes to a close and gives way to the race. The day of the race will indicate how the months of training went, and will tell it to you straight. If you've been honest with yourself, it should come as no surprise. You can take shortcuts in training, and they may make those training days easier, but they will probably not make race day easier. Whether your training plan was good or bad - or if you stuck to it - will become evident. Race day is judgment day, and there's no hiding from the choices you made in getting there. Sure, you can hide them from other people: most fans and other racers don't really know what you're capable of, but you sure do.

Sometimes the other racers help illustrate your choices. I remember starting my first marathon amidst a field of tens of thousands, after a tough season of training gently on the borderline of getting stronger while managing a painful injury. My strategy was a slow-and-steady run-walk pace, and let me tell you: when my watch beeped after the first eight minutes and I slowed to a walk aside six lanes of bodies rushing past me like the mighty Mississippi, it was tough to believe in my plan. It took a lot of faith to predict the sweetness I would feel three hours later, moving up through the field, as the pace that was most appropriate for me on that day actualized itself into my version of success.

Some die-hard runners insist that it didn't count because I didn't run the whole thing, but I went 26.2 miles. I'm sure that among the people I passed at the end were at least a few who took some short cuts in their training, or made excuses to themselves or others, or lost the discipline to rest or eat right. Race day hammered down its impartial gavel in response.

The long races call your values to the table right within the race. Do you know yourself well enough to spend just the right amount of energy during the swim and bike to be able to run your best? Have you exercised the patience required to do your best - through the morning and through the season? Have you stuck to your plans and also adapted on the fly to the inevitable changes that have arisen? In life it can be tempting to make excuses when things don't go our way; if we sit and pout on race day, the clock still keeps on ticking.

I like to see people enjoy success at the races - it's disappointing to see dreams come apart with cramps, overheating, GI problems, and who knows what else. But there was a certain feeling of vindication halfway through that Ironman marathon run, as I trotted along past other athletes collapsing as some earlier impatience came running up and grabbed them from behind. I have no knowledge of their situations, their training, or their personal composition, but the notion that some athletes break down speaks loudly enough to me about my own choices. An athlete can stand at the starting line and boast about his or her speed or time or equipment - and some do. I try to quietly let these remarks just roll on by, because the race will speak for itself. I feel safe and optimistic knowing that although I can't overpower a bully, the race will beat up the cocky contestant who fails to respect it, and move the patient believer steadily up through the field and across the line.

Seldom is credit given out loud for holding true to important values. For trying extra hard, or making choices that aren't immediately rewarding; for going after the goals that seem ultimately important. On race day, all the hard work and the faith give way to the truth - the proof - and you end up with a medal around your neck that says *"you were brave, you did not compromise your values, you achieved your goals."* In each medal, each finish line, the race itself presents an opportunity to get credit for character.

A TALE OF TRIATHLON AND FOOTBALL

Memorial Union Terrace is one of Madison's most quintessential spaces. The back patio of the University's main student union sits on the shore of Lake Mendota, the upper and larger lake bounding our top-rated, health-conscious isthmus. This community gathering place is mostly dotted with students during the days, studying or socializing, but packed in the summer evenings with everyone. I've felt inspiration sitting here writing on sunny afternoons; there's just something so pleasing about the lake, to look at and be next to. It's about three miles across, so on most days the entire shoreline is visible, and the distant trees on the opposite shore provide a calming backdrop to whatever activity unfolds among the iconic yellow, orange, and green chairs and tables of the Union.

Madison's lakes are essential to its identity, both in their natural beauty and in the activities they host. Madison sits on an isthmus - a small strip of land between two lakes - the larger Mendota to the North and the smaller Monona to the South. Many more lakes dot the region and play host to all kinds of enjoyment. Fishing is popular here, both as a pastime and a means of putting food on the table. Wintertime brings sizeable shanty towns of ice-fishing shacks on the lakes, and folks sitting on buckets with lines in the water. The process is essential to Wisconsin's cultural identity - but I'm not sure that for many, actually bringing any fish home is a higher priority than being outside, feeling connected to the earth, being with friends, and soaking up the scarce hours with loved ones, as slowly as possible.

One particular winter day, a couple teammates and I passed the frozen village on the longest training run of our season, in preparation for a February marathon. We had completed a 13-mile lap all the way around Lake Monona and were heading around the bay before heading back in: *seven more miles* to go. "Perseverance" was the primary objective. It was a lovely sunny day, but a winter afternoon so cold that the bright sunlight brought no glimpse of melting anywhere. According to protocol, we had dressed in layers that morning, but had never taken a single one of them off.

We were chatting about the phenomenon of the ice fishing shanty town as we ran around it - and I was noticing the big pickup trucks and tough flannel-clad men, women, and children hanging around. Offering a couple "good mornings" as we passed, I wondered what they thought of us in our form-fitting stretchy moisture-wicking technical fabrics, running around in the snow. I noticed my mind applying stereotypes - big trucks honking or blasting exhaust onto a line of cyclists in the countryside - but also noticed that such a judgment would be a fallacy.

Here, we're all toughing out the cold weather to be outside doing things important to us. We're all trying to get the most out of this gorgeous day, even at the cost of some discomfort. I want to say "good morning, we are running 20 miles" to be sure the people we pass know just what we are going through. I want to say to all the sportsmen - from hunters to cyclists - *hey, the outdoors are here for all kinds of sports, if we all care for it.* We have more in common than it may appear... to a closed mind.

As a triathlete, the lakes are an essential place for our version of play - training and racing. Since agriculture lives so close to the city, there's a noticeably audible call around town for measures like runoff control to preserve the clean quality of the lakes. Runoff water that picks up phosphorous from fertilizers in fact fertilizes algae in the lakes, making them weedy and making a swimmer susceptible to a day of really uncomfortable GI distress. When summer finally arrives and the water is warm enough for jumping in - when I can finally "go somewhere" instead of following a monotonous 25-yard black line - I hope that it will be clean and uninhibited.

Even more so, the weeds become a huge barrier when I encourage a new tri teammate to venture into the open water for the first time. It can be scary enough to head face-down into a lake without a wall to hang on to, let alone getting tangled up in algae. My favorite beach often ends up closed much of the summer for "elevated levels of blue-green algae," and while I'm neither here to harp on environmental policy nor complain, I'm disappointed when interests compete like enjoying a day on the lake and feeding the population. I suspect the anglers would tend to agree.

***

I like the university town. There's a lot of energy, a lot of things going on, a lot of people out and about. I think I particularly notice the love for football because my college experience was missing any semblance of athletics-based school pride. I don't regret my name being on the Dean's list, or the list of Society of Civil Engineers chapter presidents, or even the list of Glee Club presidents. My rockin' a cappella group was sadly ahead of its time. I did get out of my room at least a little bit, just never to go to a football game.

I tried to get a bit of exercise - riding my bike or rollerblading across campus, playing racquetball. But sports just weren't my cup of tea, I didn't feel like I could be qualified to be on any kind of a team, even intramural. I wanted to be in shape, I wanted to be good-looking, but I just didn't know how, and it wasn't high enough on my priority list to merit a lot of my attention. I don't know if my college had a triathlon team... I do sometimes wonder what life might be like today had I discovered the sport 10 years ago.

No one I hung around with at school really talked about football - it wasn't a big uniting bond. The entire student body of my little division-3 school would fit into Wisconsin's stadium... about 7 times. So while I did have things in common with other students I knew, there weren't many things uniting the whole student body. The university looked for ways to make this possible, and even made significant investments into a football field just after I graduated. Certain things brought together the engineering school, or the medical school, or one group or another, but there weren't days when the entire student body - and local alumni and local businesses and everyone else in town - was all wearing the same color in solidarity. I later adopted an alma mater I never had - at least on game day. The uniting energy is a lot of fun.

One summer night, I went to the Union Terrace to hear a band, created by a friend and composed of an unlikely collection of local musicians with otherwise-respectable PhD-wielding daytime gigs. Their classic rock covers were stellar, and I was having a great time relaxing, listening, and watching all the people. It was not only a great summer evening out, but also the eve of a game day. A few folks wore shirts and caps with the visitors' logo - some had made a 2,000-mile journey to support their team. A pretty excellent commitment, if you ask me... but it turned out to be risky.

At one point between songs, the singer rallied the crowd with some words to everyone, generally indicating that the home team would win the next day, if you get my drift - pretty much pointing at the other-colored-shirt wearers to say "watch out, you're in enemy territory here!" Poking fun - not too harsh, but not too nice. The university encourages residents to be welcoming to their visitors, but shirts in our colors and bearing expressions like "eat sh*t" are also available. A moment later, the crowd at the Terrace, otherwise chilling out and loving the summer afternoon, suddenly united in a repetitive and simple jeer to the visitors, not fit for print but referring to a certain end of the digestive system whose two-syllable name can be called out back and forth between two groups of fans. Another level of the unification that football brings to this town is the unfortunate but common vocabulary of vulgar and downright mean chants and sayings.

And here is where I began to consider distinct differences between this fun and widely-uniting game of football and "my sports" like marathon-running and triathlon. Not everything I see printed on tri-related T-shirts is positive, but even an image of, say, cartoon racers vomiting send a message more like "Ha, I am puking!" than "I hope you do." When the big tri comes to Madison, the crowd of athletes is diverse and representative of many different states and nations; all sorts of super-dedicated fans make long journeys to be there to support their athletes on this momentous day. The races bring entire families to the roadside, posting banners and dressing in custom-printed shirts with their athlete's name or sayings. It's a blast to read what some of these people come up with - and it's a moving demonstration of support.

When I did my first iron-distance race in 2009, I was blown away by the efforts my family made to support me. They wore matching T-shirts, hung a huge banner, and planted signs on the big climbs, bearing lyrics to my favorite motivational songs. All this after traveling from the edges of the country to watch one day of racing. But it was the experience of getting up early to watch the race the following year that really drove it home for me. I was terribly excited and could barely keep from running, even though more than an hour buffered my arrival from the race start. When I paused to look around the otherwise sleeping city, all around were families much like mine: they were dressed in uniform, carrying signs and balloons and their athletes' tire pumps and extra gear. They were alive with excitement and laughter and diligent planning, checking pace charts and plotting out the best course for seeing their hero go by. For the first time, I could see it objectively, away from the focus required of a participating racer, and zoomed out from the view of just my own family.

The first tears of the day began to roll.

The course is lined with jubilant supporters, and although they are committed to helping their athlete cross the line, they don't waste their energy on discouraging words for whoever crosses the line later. In fact, some of the biggest cheers come for those who finish the very last. As the last swimmers make their way to the beach and the 2-hour-20-minute time cutoff approaches, all the course lifeguards surround that athlete, amidst a din from the race announcer and the fans. If that athlete doesn't make the cutoff - and often only one or two do not - I can say with confidence that no one chants obscenities, but rather shower that person with praise for their courage to start, and encouragement to try again. As the clock approaches midnight - the 17-hour benchmark ending the race - the crowd's intensity far exceeds the noise some nine hours prior, when the first "winner" finished. It's refreshing that (except, perhaps in the rare instance of cheating) the sport's vernacular just won't tolerate calling someone "loser."

On the course, the vibe is no different. Sure, it's important for a few athletes to finish in front of others in order to earn rankings or prize money, or qualification spots at higher-level races. But one athlete finishes in front of another not so much by beating the other, but by having more to offer the race on that day. When I do well in my age group but do not win, it's simply because the other guys were faster than me that day. When I'm feeling competitive, it's a great motivation to try to stay in front, but at the bottom line, I only have so much to offer on race day - and so does the other guy - and eventually someone's 100% is a little faster than someone else's.

The athletes who compete in long-distance races would rather encourage each other to do their best and let the best one win than to try to beat down the other to gain a leg up. At the world championships in 2008, when the women's leader was stopped at the side of the road with a flat tire and no air canister left to inflate it, the second place competitor dropped one for her. She repaired the flat and came back to win the race - because the sportsmanship to empower everyone to compete at their very best trumps the willingness to let bad luck keep the better athlete from winning.

Watch the end of an iron-distance triathlon, especially one that concludes with a neck-and-neck finish, where two individuals give everything they have - nearing the end of an *eight hour* race. The professionals who go after first place have to take huge chances at the edge of their physical and mental limits. To stay in front, they don't let up for a second, even in a race that requires intense patience and pacing. At the end of this very spectacle of human endurance, there's nothing left. But watch what happens after first place comes across the line and is named the champion: he stands and waits until second place comes in, and they embrace and congratulate each other. They don't tap hands in some kind of half-shake, either, they cry on each other. They embrace and thank each other for the race. The positives of the accomplishment itself are the only thing relevant: there is no rooting "against" anyone, only the celebration of each athlete giving his or her very best to do on that day whatever they set out to do.

Something gets badly missed when focus shifts away from encouragement, away from lifting up and toward beating down. The us-versus-them concept is so deeply ingrained in our systems, it's hard to overcome. Even at the Team In Training inspiration dinner the night before the Green Bay Marathon, participants from Wisconsin and Minnesota exchanged taunts on the basis of their football rivalries - probably without even realizing. Indeed, on race day, the race itself - or perhaps a personal best - is the only thing you're "against," if you must call it that. Wouldn't it be a bummer for a triathlon to have one "winner" and 1,999 "losers?" Each race can be filled with so many more victories when each person celebrates both their own and everyone else's.

RACE REPORT:
ATHENS MARATHON

In the fall of 2010, I went on a pilgrimage. It was a once-in-a-lifetime opportunity to commemorate probably the only 2,500th anniversary of anything that I will ever live to see: the Athens Marathon. In 490 BCE, the underdog Athenians won a critical battle against the attacking Persians at the Battle of Marathon. As legend has it, a soldier-messenger named Pheidippides ran back home from Marathon to Athens, about 25 miles away, to proclaim the good news "Nikomen!" ("we have won!") ... and dropped dead.

Certainly the stigma of the modern marathon was born of this heroic run and perfectly-scripted collapse. (Note to any ultra-marathoners reading, if the 25-miler wasn't enough, Pheidippides had also allegedly run some 240k back and forth to Sparta already!) Around the time I was finishing the Mardi Gras Marathon in February and considering what the heck I could possibly do next after such a high, I noticed that the race tracing that original route - and used in the first modern Olympic games in 1896 - was about to open for registration. So what if it was in Greece? A detail to solve later. It wasn't something to miss - so I registered. As best I could tell, anyway, what with the website being only somewhat in English.

I went to Athens having finished four marathons, including one nestled at the end of a triathlon. I had a tremendous respect for the distance, and the incredible emotions it evokes. Part of what continues to draw me to this magical distance is the strange and surreal high that develops with the decision to persevere through intense fatigue and impossible doubt. In my journey of becoming an "athlete," I've done a lot of considering what we learn about ourselves and our lives through the races. I set out on this transatlantic journey to a place so rich with history (*the birthplace of democracy, for crying out loud!*) that I figured there would simply be no way around being overwhelmed with a transcendent connection with the history of the place. I thought that during the meditation of run-miles, I would empathize with Pheidippides, or be somehow transported to his historical setting and experience.

But it wasn't quite like that. What I found wasn't myself living in the legend of 490 B.C., it was something more relevant - something even more timeless.

I had not been in the Newark airport for an hour when I spotted a purple bracelet and struck up a conversation with a fellow Team in Training alum on her way to the race. As passengers took their seats, it didn't take more than a couple minutes for the conversations to begin - to realize that the entire 767 was full of runners. Unlike the typical quiet that settles over a plane as it prepares to depart, the place was alive with the buzz of race stories and the anticipation of Athens. A glance down the aisle revealed all the modern running-shoe brands.

Around the city of Athens, the streets were noticeably alive with a special group of tourists, sporting Boston jackets and Finisher hats and technical-fabric shirts in all kinds of languages. At lunch Saturday we spotted a group of Chinese runners, looking particularly professional in their warm-up clothes. As soon as I took out my camera to snatch a picture of them, they motioned and insisted that we all take photos together. Athens, I believe, is as close as I will ever feel to being in the Olympics.

The day before the race, I took a bus tour of the course. I arrived at the stadium in Marathon just as a ceremony was wrapping up, where young men and women, sharply dressed in their country's military best, met each other before competing in an international championship as part of the marathon. To the side of the stadium, the Olympic flame burned in a glistening silver dish atop a stone staircase, and as we stood next to it to take photos, a young man asked if I would take his photo with the flame. Of course I did; he asked where I was from, and seemed to be thrilled to be talking to an American. With a huge smile, he told me he was from Germany, and eager to run in the next day's championship.

In the quiet of the 25-mile bus trip back, I couldn't help but think that barely two generations ago, he and I might have tried to kill each other on a battlefield. Instead, this weekend we had the privilege of sharing a starting and finish line, each doing battle with none other than himself, with each other's support rather than fear and hatred.

On race morning, I was delighted, but honestly not surprised, to come up the escalator at 5:00 a.m. in Athens, Greece, and see purple shirts. Individuals like me - alumni sporting our colors in dedication to the Team - and groups as well, like "Greece Lightning" from Texas, had raised money and trained together for this significant race. As a charity runner, I often hear various thanks along the way, but to hear them in Marathon made me very proud. Proud to recognize that if a person speaks American English, when they see purple they shout "Go Team!" Proud to realize that the sport of modern marathoning would not be what it is without the empowering powerhouse of Team in Training, accepting anybody who wants to dream about a finish line and watching them earn a medal around their neck. Proud to know that we fund research that lets someone who once heard their doctor say "I'm sorry, you have cancer," later go to Athens in the footsteps of Pheidippides, both of whom can proclaim "we have won" 42.2k later, but only one of whom dies at the end of the story.

As 12,500 runners assembled on a sunny Sunday morning and met each other in the shadow of the Olympic flame and a long row of the world's flags, the race organizers welcomed us. The president of the race organization said "The Marathon symbolizes, not only for the humanity but also for hundreds of marathon runners from all over the globe, the values of peace, the fellowship of nations, the importance of human feats and the need of people for great, truthful, and good ideals, this is applied not only in their athletic activities but also in their everyday lives." The Mayor of Athens concurred that the Marathon "is a tribute to the human will, a race-challenge for the human soul, a race that goes beyond the limits of a simple sport event." And with a gunshot that contained no bullet, runners from around the world set out with a common and peaceful goal.

I ran a smart race. I checked the forecasts and dressed right, memorized the grades, ate right in preparation and throughout the race, took on nutrition and water, kept my sodium levels up and avoided cramping, cooled myself off with water when I got hot, and walked when I needed a break. I minded my effort level on the long climbs and minded my form on the few descents. A blue line permanently painted on the road signifies the Olympic route, supplemented by shining blue road signs to "Athina." Keeping a casual eye on the clock, I got great satisfaction from how much faster each kilometer comes than a mile, and eventually began to really believe and kick in the last 10k to negative split and bring home a PR in the end. My goal was not to push myself toward a PR in this hot, hilly, historic event - I wanted instead to make the most of the day. In the race, though, I realized that to push was truly to make the most of the day: I owed it to this race to give it everything I had. The stuff of legends doesn't come from modest efforts. It was in the latest miles, when I struggled the most to keep running, that I felt the deepest connection to the race.

The setting was unique and the topography was

challenging, and I could write pages about the mile-by-mile ongoings, but this isn't what made Athens memorable. When I go back to the course in my mind, I see country names and flags on the backs of shirts. I smile thinking of dozens of runners in togas and bare feet, some bearing swords and helmets and shields. And best of all, I see the entire 42.2 kilometer route - through what first looked like dry, desolate and even abandoned rural scenes - coming alive lined with Greek people, graciously hosting us and cheering "bravo!" Children and old ladies and everyone in between confirmed their welcome by waving olive branches over the passing runners.

Sometimes I sense the shadow of a doubt, that when I describe certain experiences in these hyperbolae that I'm just dreaming and making more of something than is really there. I consider whether my sense of wonder will wear off, though I doubt it. I love to be a part of a Team in Training participant's journey through training and across their first finish line because finishing a marathon changes things, and I find energy in just being close to the same sense of wonder in someone else. Once in a while I come across other runners that don't seem to connect with the sport anything like I do, like they are just going through the motions, or are even upset or unhappy. I think Athens was unique because the field was made up of people with such reverence for the marathon that they made the long pilgrimage to honor it with their participation.

People had come to be a part of history, to be part of something so obviously very big that it was okay to let it be big. Okay to feel waves of emotions rather than try to hide them, because this historic race setting was a safe place for age-old emotions to be realized. A cultural wall seemed to be taken down, exposing a more tender humanity. After I bowed to let a short Greek woman place my heavy golden medal around my neck, wiping my tears to take in the stone stadium around me, I noticed the man next to me: a tall, beautifully fit quintessential German man - weeping. Other runners dropped to their knees, kissing the track.

I'll tell you what: that's the legend of Marathon. Two and a half millennia have no bearing on the timeless truths that the marathon stands testament to. The resilience of the human spirit. The inability of fear and worldly struggles to get in the way of the great achievements that dreamers turn into reality through their commitments. On top of everything the marathon means to the individuals who run it, it also creates a bond among them, which on this day included all the world, and reminded me again and again that the human spirit itself is not bounded by black lines on a globe, but bonded by the blue line on the road.

Mark Twain astutely wrote that "travel is fatal to prejudice, bigotry, and narrow-mindedness." So if world peace is indeed our dream, then let our challenge be to go out into the world, understand the people who inhabit its other corners, and be peaceful.

If Pheidippides was indeed just a legend, on this day he was certainly actualized in the hearts of the runners who came to know him over his famous route. But instead of honing the implements of war, we strengthened the elegant machine of the human body and the delicate bonds between the world's people that have far more in common than some may want to believe. Especially on this day, when the raw power of the marathon challenge unites us. Nikomen!

A CASE FOR SPACE

I decided to ring in the new year at a midnight yoga class. Upside down. Glance at your calendar: what's the date today? Were you planning to make new year's resolutions? How are they going so far? The truth is, you don't really need to wait for a new year to make a resolution or try to improve some part of your life. Sometimes inspiration comes from happening upon an event and feeling a mysterious desire to try it yourself. Often it comes from a friend's encouragement; sometimes it comes from the depths of intense change or loss. I guess I might seem like the kind of guy who likes to try new things - but I haven't always been, and it's only because certain opportunities opened up to me in which I felt bold enough to try.

It takes a lot of guts to try something new. Often, it's not even trying the thing itself that holds us back, but the other people already doing it. To try out an exercise class, to take your new bike to a group ride, to slip into a lane at the pool, to join a team to train for an event completely foreign to anything you have tried, even to start a new job: these attempts can be terrifying! Just stepping through the door requires getting past a deluge of mental barriers shouting "What if I don't know what to do / what if I don't fit in / what if people make fun of me / *what if I fail?*' We've all been in those anxious, reluctant situations in one way or another.

For the past several years, every four months I kicked off a new Team In Training season. As the coach, I was one of the people already standing inside the decorated room, wearing the logo T-shirt, when someone new showed up to tentatively inquire. They came from all different backgrounds, and often greeted me with doubts and disclaimers, to which I replied with blind faith, thanks, and encouragement. Maybe some arrived on the impetus of New Year's resolutions - but I'm guessing that most were just "regular" resolutions. Regardless of who they were, I wanted to help them immediately begin moving toward whatever they defined as success. I asked about their goals, showed them the program, and answered their questions. When I became a leader, it was my role to maintain a construct of space for new participants to begin and cultivate their journey.

Whether or not we consider ourselves leaders, wherever we have experience *we* are the ones already there. We are the ones who know what we're doing, already in the middle of the routine, who a beginner must encounter. The one already swimming laps up and down the middle of the lane. The one already laying on our back on a yoga mat with our eyes closed, pretending to be oblivious to the next person coming into the room in hopes that we won't have to move for them. The one already experienced in running and ready to go off the front at the pace that challenges us during an all-abilities-welcome group run. If we're not careful, we might just be the barrier to someone else's entry. Who can we offer a welcome? Where can you make more space?

Because you never know who might need it. You never know what they might be able to do with it. You never know who might be ready to finally take the first step to turning their life around - to getting in shape, losing weight, gaining all the empowerment and joy that triathlon - or whatever - has to offer. Some of the greatest athletes were put down when they initially tried; so were some of the greatest inventors and business people. One friend and mentor was told, when first inquiring about running shoes, that he was too big to run; he has since competed in Kona at the World Championship. I remember middle school classmates shouting at me during some inconsequential gym class soccer game: "Tyler, you scrub!" It took a long time - and a certain proverbial primordial soup of encouragement - to realize that I actually had potential in a certain part of the foreign world of "athletics." It took a combination of my own drive and others making just enough room for me to get started.

***

I can think of a day when many things went very badly for me, when my heart sank and my body felt weak; my usual enthusiasm deflated. I remember wanting to get out of my cold, silent house and into a safe place where I wouldn't have to be so alone, but could just… be. Only in the stillness of each long breath did I feel the tiniest comfort just in being alive enough to breathe it. It's really not too hard to imagine. The day a loved one went away, from some place or from this earth; the day something broke that will never be repaired; the strange and directionless empty mornings in the days following something very big. Stop for a moment: can you remember a day like this?

I mustered the courage to pick myself up and go out to one of my favorite yoga classes. The class looked no different than usual - including my presence, which was regular there. Except this time, instead of being early to this popular class, I tiptoed into an already-full room and squeezed in between a couple other mats already unrolled. I didn't want to talk to anyone, I didn't want to explain myself. I just wanted to be in the warm room, doing something that made me feel good in many ways - or at least feel normal - and hopefully feel the presence of the other people around me as a collective uplifting energy.

A couple more people came in after me, although the room

appeared already full. Where might they have come from that they too might crave this space? What might they need to heal - and who am I to say that they shouldn't? Eventually the meditative silence was broken when a fellow student said what was already in my mind, "come on, let's make some more room." Someone must have been meditating on compassion, and decided that calling for inclusion was more important than silently thinking about it. How often is there more space - more abundance - than the group acknowledges; how much more space is there, in fact, for others who need to share it?

We're challenged to make space for others, but need also to make space for ourselves. Running, biking or swimming - especially outside - can create a space to find a special kind of comfort. It can be a reprieve from day-to-day life - an escape from the expectations of work, parenting, or other obligations. I like to set out in the early morning hours, as the sunrise illuminates the sky in changing shades of blue and orange and the early-birds sing their joyful songs. I find a freedom in empty streets and flashing yellow signals, unencumbered by incessant traffic traveling at lethal speeds, texting to boot. I feel safely isolated as a little head bobbing in the middle of a lake, the shore and all its tasks safely in the distance.

Although life seems to ask us to simultaneously run scattered in different directions, it is our challenge to choose which directions we want to go, and go firmly. One of the best parts of those early morning workouts is the practice of mono-tasking: just being where I am. Focusing on one thing at a time means doing it intentionally, and doing it well. It translates to making space to evaluate priorities, think, or rest; it inspires the skill of focusing empathetically on the people you are talking or interacting with. Intentionally clearing away noise creates a good place for listening.

Here, many people's workouts become spiritual journeys. The physical effort combined with a certain clarity of mind makes space for a different way of looking at the world. Out there, we can get into a place where we can connect with concepts, perceive notions of a deeper reality, get abstract, or feel pushed by something that isn't even there. It's where I've perceived this entire text, trapped in some other dimension and waiting for me to access it and write it down onto this page. It's where I've previewed key races - both by practicing on the course itself, and visualizing the same place in a setting that does not yet exist, across the transcendent border of time.

There are more dimensions to this life - more ways to look at the world - than initially meet the eye, and our challenge is to create the space to find them. Likewise, the other people our lives share the world with are full of potential that we sometimes play a role in unlocking. On the road, in a room, at a race, at an event: where can we be more generous with what we mistakenly think is totally full? What do we love so much that we would be remiss to deny it to someone else, even if it means going a little bit out of our way to accommodate them?

I'm glad that I have these outlets to find comfort in hard times, and thoughtfulness in good times alike. I also want others to have the same outlet; I see no reason to deny anyone an opportunity for healing or joyfulness. If exclusion slips into the very routines that give us freedom - or into any of our attitudes - maybe we should reconsider what it is we're practicing.

A DIFFERENT KIND OF READY

I came off my first iron-distance race with a great high, then a relaxing off-season. As the next summer blossomed, I competed at local races in a not-so-structured manner, and lived the proverbial "multisport lifestyle." I woke up early, ate well, and worked out because it made me feel good. Who did I hang around with? People who related to terms like "triathlete" or "runner" - and those who I coached who were just beginning to realize that they, too, fit these categories. What did I do in my spare time? I "trained."

Something inside me had advised against signing up for such a big race a second year in a row. The opportunity only lasts a moment: a long line forms the morning after race day, and after the doors open at 9 in the morning, it clears away quickly, leaving the race sold-out a year in advance. I had a slight sense of regret as other athletes signed up and I hobbled my way past, to the merchandise shop then back home - but it turned out to be a good decision.

When something comes into life that is truly unlike any other experience, it can be wise to take some time away from it, to digest it and look at it from a different angle, before jumping in again. When something demands a lot of time and effort, space away from it can be rejuvenating enough that on a second approach, the commitment doesn't feel like a burden. Even life's best experiences aren't quite the same when experienced a second time - but with some attention, they can have a very special meaning of their own.

I thought I might have enjoyed not following a rigidly-structured training plan. It sounded fun to try just getting out there - playing outside. Close friends have advised me that I could benefit from being more relaxed. So I tried it, and discovered that the structure of a schedule is, in fact, entirely liberating: it's a lot easier to train when you know what your goals are. Most notably, when "rest" is specifically programmed into a schedule, nestled carefully between periods of intensity for the specific purpose of recovery, it's easier to take.

Rest, without residing on a schedule, can feel more like a mistake - a void where something could or should be happening, but isn't. When rest is intentional and deliberate, that time can be set aside for something else - one of the many endeavors that otherwise ends up taking a bitter back seat to the training deluge. Taking the time to rest, step back, and focus on something else for a change is wonderfully refreshing, both to the muscles and to the soul.

If I believed in my schedule - which I did - then I could believe in the rest periods and know that everything I had built would still be waiting for me when I returned. When I set up my first year-long training schedule, I made the periods of rest and recovery coincide with my vacations. The following year, of course I still went on vacations, but often felt a need to take running clothes: *maybe* I'd wake up early to train. It's fun to get out and explore on foot, burning off some of the lethargy that celebration can bring - but some days might be better spent sleeping in, or sitting still with a big cup of hot coffee. Without a plan, I often felt guilty no matter which I chose, unsure whether I had chosen the right one for the day.

When race day came back at the end of the year, I got to play the role of spectator and observer as many of my friends participated. I got to experience being a veteran; I wore my finisher's hat. I tried to stay entirely supportive, and bite my tongue as friends told me of their grand plans. This was not my race, these were not my goals. In my approach, I don't focus much on the clock - but that doesn't mean that someone else shouldn't, or that even if they do, it would take anything away from me. It's every person for themselves, goofy strategies and all. On race day, I arrived downtown well before the starting cannon, and stayed into the night, too excited to pull myself away.

***

I didn't exactly choose to sign up again. I found myself awake well before dawn and taking my place in that momentous sign-up line for the second time. Just as it called me to try it before, it called me back again. That dark, chilly September morning was in many ways just as it was two years prior - but I was a different person. I knew things I didn't know before.

I had a whole carafe of coffee, a folding camp chair, a blanket and ample snacks to share. As others took their seats around me, I introduced myself and started conversation. This time, they were the sheepish first-timers, and to them I was the old pro. I practiced listening rather than talking quite so much - avoiding giving advice except when asked - and felt refreshed hearing the beginners' perspective. Honestly, I think it was even better from the "other side."

Again, I trained for a year, but it had a different flavor. I came into it with a different level of baseline experience, skill, and confidence. Along the way I dealt with a whole new set of stressors, and responded to them with what feels like a whole new mindset. Some of my races arrived with good preparation, but without big fanfare. When they did, I wondered: was I still growing? Did I have a larger goal beyond the end-of-season A-race itself? As I made my way through another year, my biggest races remained the focus of my training, but not the primary focus of my entire life.

Admittedly, from one year to the next, I've gotten better at racing. Especially in the short courses, I turned in faster and faster times, and often ranked nearer the front of the pack. However, I didn't think my training was always as intense. I began to wonder whether I was getting substantially stronger, or whether I was just developing a better aptitude for racing, and a higher comfort level with pushing harder. My faith in myself has dramatically improved and as such, I can get more out of my own body before I feel the absolute need to back off. I have a new tolerance for pain.

Committing to something new and exciting is relatively easy because the intense desire to explore it easily consumes the entire mind. It leaves less room for second-guessing how else I might be spending my time. In my second time around, I had more experience with the course, my equipment, my own body, my friends and opportunities. On all of these were the benchmarks that all my prior experiences have left on the wall. The first time is new territory - it has nothing to be judged against; the second time has the opportunity to be "better." Especially in a setting like racing, with its specific numerical results, it's tempting to think that each subsequent event will only be worthwhile if it is "better" than the previous.

If you're in tune with who you are and what you want overall, it's a lot easier to choose from all of life's directions. Sure, there will be bumps and recalculations along the way, but the overarching goals - what could be called values - help guide the smaller decisions. Life deals me new situations that I have never seen before, and just as in racing, I react from the foundation of inner strength and adaptability that I have developed. If you don't know who you are or what you want, at least heading in a direction may give you some idea. It doesn't have to be perfect to be meaningful; pick one and see where it takes you. Trying to head in all directions will just pull you apart.

These notions transcend racing. They permeate the things we pursue most heartily: relationships, jobs, traditions. In spite of our best efforts, even the most steadfast of these necessarily change from year to year, and it's up to us to approach them relevant to where we are, and find the best in them. In my year of training the second time around, I experienced a significant relationship change, and I wondered: after such a loss, could I ever feel "new" love again? Would I be forever jaded and never able to commit in quite the same way?

I decided to take a lesson from the races: of course I could. I'd have to accept where I came from, understanding that previous "results" were only a partial indicator of what my future self might become. I'd have to be open to the ways that a new experience would be different, even if it initially looked the same as something I'd done before. Only in knowing that it must be different could I let it be its own and avoid judging it against previous incarnations. I know how to adjust to the conditions; I know how to draw on my past experience, but not live in it at the expense of the good things right in front of me.

Just as I evolved from "novice" to "experienced," my equipment transformed from "new" to "trusty." When race days come around, I grab the same trusty stuff. But each time, it's sponge-bathed, lubed and polished. New gear can be a great motivator to step up and be the level of athlete who deserves it, but old gear can still do just the same with respect. With good care and maintenance, gear can keep looking and performing like new. With ongoing love that refuses to become complacent, something dear will remain as valuable with time as it was at first sight.

Once the trucks showed up and the city began to transform into race-mode, I was overcome with excitement for my second time. This time, I was also able to sleep the last few nights leading up to the race - perhaps proving that although I was excited, I was not too anxious. Sure, it would be a tough day, but having done it before, having been active in the two years since, and having trained diligently, my subconscious was convinced that there was no need to doubt. I did what I could do, and I was as ready as I was going to be. Nobody's ever really ready for a race like this - anything can happen. But I know my way around a triathlon, and felt like I had a lot of risks managed. I was ready to take it on.

The first time, I was venturing into completely uncharted territory, and I absolutely had to succeed. The second time, it was still big, and uncharted to a large degree, and still important, but somehow a bit more like a big, tough, fun event than a critical definition of my persona. In writing about the journey, I've watched myself more objectively; coaching other athletes also gave me new perspective into the minds of people at the races. Being around the pre-race crowd gathering in Madison gave me a tremendous satisfaction in knowing that I have, in fact, completed this race before. I'm not a novice - but in my second time around, I was a novice at being a veteran.

Perhaps the toughest part of the second time is trying to retain all the positive feelings of the first time. Being a beginner is being wide-eyed and open-mouthed, staring up into the sky in incredulity, gladly disregarding anything that does not contribute to the greatness of the "new" experience. Patience and joy come easier to a beginner because other forces have not been allowed to question them. To find the deepest, truest joy in experiences, we must set aside preconceptions, inflated egos, and past experiences to approach them with an open mind - the beginner's mind.

As I calmly philosophize on the imminent race, I remember that it's the first big race for many athletes, just as it once was for me. They're nervous, and I'm casually rounding up my tried-and-true gear. They're laser-focused and telling all their friends, and in a way I'm preparing for a vacation. In another way, in spite of my experience, I'm intensely excited, and yes, a little nervous. If I'm complacent with a long race like this, I know I'll have a lousy day - but I'll stick to my checklists, remembering that my organizational skills finally have found a good sporting-home.

I'll stick to smiling throughout. As the race unfolds, I'll watch it with wide-open eyes to see how my body reacts on the particular day, the second time around. What used to be intense jitters have transformed into less-nervous but still-excited childlike incredulity. I feel ready. My bags are packed, my bike is sponge-bathed and glistening. I'm shaved and tapered. We're off to the races.

RACE REPORT:
IRONMAN WISCONSIN 2011

What a day. Race-morning weather set the stage: about 55 degrees, and perfectly calm. "You can't pick the weather on race day," but if I got to pick, this would be it. A couple weeks before the race, the highs were in the mid-90's; in the two days leading up to the race a steady wind whipped up whitecaps on the lakes. I skipped my final training swims because I didn't need the GI and immune system stress of extra mouthfuls of lake water, and didn't have a great desire to get any more practice swimming against adverse conditions. If I have to on race day, I just do what it takes. Before the race, I didn't have to. A picturesque sunrise over a crystal clear blue sky set the backdrop for a slowly-sung and heartfelt National Anthem as the last athletes - including me - eased into the water.

Out of about 2,500 athletes preparing for the mass start, I found myself right next to one particular friend who interestingly seemed to show up next to me at some point in practically every race I did this year! *Race like you train*, I guess. The cannon blew, and I started out slowly, way off to the right, and way off in the back. Over the years I've become more confident and calm in the water, but I'm still not a strong swimmer, and there's no need to push it. In a race like this, a couple minutes are well worth the opportunity to find my rhythm with a little extra space. One of my new tricks for staying calm on the swim is singing as I go along (thanks, Nicole!) - though it's hard to find songs with tempos as slow as my stroke. The one I keep coming back to again and again is Strauss' "Blue Danube" waltz. (By the time I came out of the water an hour and a half later, even this 10-minute super-classic was getting a little tired).

The first half-lap set a good tone: I could hear the fans beside the water, and see them stacked up on Monona Terrace. When I was alongside my family, I could see their huge banner, and I gave them a big wave mid-stroke, and saw them jumping up and down in response. I had a bit of trouble with water leaking into my goggles, which I had kept really loose to try to ward off a potential headache, but a quick pull on the strap took care of that for the remainder. After the madness of the first turn, I was able to find some feet and pick up a draft - wow, did that reduce my effort a ton! I had to slow down the Beautiful Blue Danube even more; my eyes were practically closing. Was I going too slow? No - I glanced at my watch, and the draft was helping me go just as fast, but with far less effort. I had to open up my eyes wide when a nearby swimmer - who I dubbed "Mr. Splashy" - kept blasting his legs next to my face.

Just before I turned the corner to head back on my second lap, a sleek black dolphin glided by beside me - the first pro finishing his swim. Which I did, too, only 40 minutes later. I followed various feet, sung songs, and tried to keep taking it easy: the swim is the warm-up. As I came out of the water, I heard two friends scream out to me: they're both accomplished photographers and were out to shoot the race. In my excitement, I instinctively brought out my jazz hands!

I walked - but quickly and confidently - through transition. I found my bag right away, in spite of having a "regular" number rather than a "rock star" one like last time; I changed my clothes efficiently. As soon as I sat down, a willing volunteer raced up to me to help with everything: I asked him to unzip my sunglass case, unscrew my can of chamois butter (I put it on by myself, mind you!), and open up my number belt. I had never met the guy, but he treated me like a king: it's just part of the magic. Another volunteer called out my bib number to yet another volunteer who had my bike off the rack waiting for me. As I put on my shoes, I saw a huge grasshopper on the ground; I asked the bike-volunteer "are you going to move it out of the way?" She said no - so I spared a second to pick it up and move it over the wall. Racing is no excuse to not look out for living things, you know. I gave a wave to my fan crew and was off for 112.

My day on the bike had begun. Coming out of the transition, I heard someone call "Dan Tyler!" (if you're reading, please identify yourself) and as I turned to wave, I clipped a traffic drum. Fortunately I didn't crash - because how lousy would that have been? If you're going to wave and go nuts, Dano, be careful. I settled in to an easy pace and started taking in the day. I felt absolutely great. After 20 minutes of just water, I turned on my timer: every 20 minutes I would try to take in food, to replenish from the swim, and fuel for the bike and upcoming run. As the day goes on, it gets harder and harder to eat, so it's important to take in a lot of calories in the first half of the bike ride. To avoid a burning stomach, I had switched to sugar-free electrolyte tablets, which I pop into my aero drink and sip, sip, sip. On a hot day like this one, I had to take in a lot of water and electrolytes to keep sweating, and keep from cramping.

Enter the SECRET WEAPON: extra-salty dried beef, which not only delivered sodium, but a welcome savory flavor amidst a day of sweet goo. Along the bottom part of the ride, where it's relatively flat, I brought it out of my pocket, unzipped the baggie, and ... YUM. It was so salty that when my brother, through-hiking the Appalachian Trail, received a package of it from my parents, he sent it back. In addition to the nutrition, it was a mental boost to know that I was deploying the SECRET WEAPON, reminding myself that I'm a nut.

Knowing where it's flat, where it's hilly, and where the water stops are located is a huge home-field advantage. I know which rollers to get out of the saddle and blast over to maintain momentum for a subsequent downhill. I know every curve of every descent, so as other riders cautiously maneuver around them, I cruise through. In a super-long race, it's fun to go 40 miles per hour the few times it's available, as a solid reminder that bicycling is fun. Climbing has always been something I've enjoyed - one nice perk to being a little guy!

At the crest of the last big hill, I got myself up to speed in anticipation of the big descent around the corner - while other riders were still riding slowly to recover from the climb. In front of me, the sag wagon had gotten caught between slow riders and spectators, unable to pass, and after following it for a moment, I decided to get moving, and went right on around it! It feels great to pass a car, and I was already up to speed when I turned the corner and went screaming like a madman down the hill. Wheeeeeeee!

I made it almost all the way to my second lap before one of the pro's lapped me. Not too shabby, I say. Staying on task and trying to keep moving, I decided to forego a bathroom break around mile 96 in Verona and just ride the last 16 miles back to Madison then go after the transition. In more fortunate weather news, the breeze had picked up (to about 15 mph), but was a tailwind for those last 16 miles home. My speed was over 20 mph, and after seeing them 8 times on the bike, I managed to beat my spreadsheet-wielding car-driving superfans back to transition. I jumped off the bike, gave it a kiss and handed it to a volunteer for re-racking, and ran in to get my run equipment.

I was feeling great, and I made a quick change into my running gear. Glad I decided to use those easy-to-pull-on compression calf guards rather than eternally-slow-to-put-on full socks! I had a shoe horn in my bag for added ease putting on my running shoes: I still like to use snug regular laces for the full marathon distance. My new shoes, socks, and sleeves glimmered white and beautiful. My GPS watch had plenty of time to locate satellites, as planned, as I ran into the restroom -

finally, after those last long 16 miles that I had decided to wait. That decision had resulted in some discomfort, but undoubtedly some added speed. Nothing motivates a person like having to get to a bathroom.

My favorite part of describing the iron-distance: "and *then* you run a marathon." There was something about it that didn't feel insurmountable, though. The momentum of the day kept me rolling forward - not feeling anxious about how far I had to go, but feeling a perpetual motion that would take me through an indefinite number of miles. I felt a calm confidence as I passed each mile marker. I suppose there could be as many mile markers as necessary - regardless of the number, I would just keep on running.

Fan support on the run course in Madison is unparalleled. From the first step, the streets were lined and people were going crazy. What a boost of energy! As I recall the run, what really comes to mind are my friends on the course. I heard "Go Team In Training" again and again. Before long, I heard my name - and I turned to the left to see one Kona-bound tri-friend on one side of the street, only to turn my head back to the right and see my family on the other. I had beaten them to T2, but they hustled back on track to catch my run.

My new lower-sugar nutrition strategy was working: I had refueled well on the bike, but wasn't having any GI distress as the run began. After a couple miles, I got to feeling really hungry, and was able to eat a couple gels. From the onset, I walked through all the water stations, taking sport drink and water at one, then cola and water at the next. Let me tell you, cola has never tasted so good - the sugar's energy and bubbles' calm went straight into me.

After several miles, I couldn't stand the sport drink any more. I made myself eat one more gel around the 1:30 mark, then just drank cola for the remainder of the day. Oh, I think I had one grape, too. It was almost a shame to pass by the smorgasbord at each water station: grapes, bananas, oranges, bars, gels, chips, pretzels, cookies, and chicken broth. As I passed through, I'd ask the volunteers "Fois gras? Caviar? Mini beef wellingtons?"

The iron-distance is truly a test of how patient you can be until the second half of the marathon. It's a delicate balance of using up a ton of energy, but saving just enough to keep running through that last 20k. With about 8 miles to go, I felt a new strength come over me - I was bringing it home. I had paced and eaten just right all day, and I knew I had enough left to run in, and run in strong. As dusk lit the road in glowing orange, many other athletes looked down at the pavement and walked slowly, but I was able to pick up the pace. I thought briefly how cool it would be to finish in 13:01, since my race number was 1301, but I was already wide open and unable to run any faster. As the sun went down and I ran the last couple miles toward home in the quiet darkness, other friends came into my mind, their spirits cheering from afar - across the country, across time, across intangible boundaries that seem to fade in the long miles and give way to a different kind of infinite presence.

And then, I was on the capitol square. My journey was ending, my carefully-crafted year-long training plan making its payoff. My patience and diligence through race week and race day - which began more than 17 hours ago when I woke up at 2:30 in the morning and was the first one online - had come to beautiful fruition. I had never looked back all day, but in that last fraction of a mile I did, because I wanted this one moment all to myself. I slowed to a jog, and slapped outstretched hands until I looked straight at the announcer in his tower, and listened proudly as he bestowed on me once again triathlon's greatest honor: "You are an Ironman!"

After the medics checked my vital signs, after receiving my medal and taking photos, after tears and tears and pizza and stretching, I sat down on a bench in a quieter place away from the commotion and just... was still. I faced the finish line and through the dense crowd watched other athletes come in, raising their arms in elation.

Out of the darkness appeared a fellow Team In Training marathon-runner and her son, who ran up to me with a big

145

smile and a hug. In the chaotic crowd, they had been hoping to see me, and somehow found my little reprieve. I was sure glad to see them. You see, this little boy had inspired me and many of my teammates. He was featured in my fundraising music video, proudly proclaiming that "when I was little, I had Leukemia, but now I'm better." He is six years old. I am nudged perpetually forward by the fans that line the course calling "Go Team!" and those countless others near and far who root for Team In Training because their lives depend on it.

How do you finish a super-long challenge? You make it bigger than yourself. You keep it in perspective, you keep it fun. You stay where you are, all day long, and avoid worrying about what's not relevant, and deal frankly with whatever comes your way. Keep on working toward your goal, no matter how long it takes. You don't have to be perfect, you have to be committed.

THE STREAK

The morning after race day brings a strange sort of quiet. All the planning yielded a big success, and the medal hangs proudly on the wall - and we have to begin coming to terms with the big event being over. But if the races play a role in defining who we are, we can't just let them go. So, invariably in the post-race quiet, we begin to write race reports, look through race photos, and look at the numbers.

I PR'd my second iron-distance triathlon by 65 minutes. *Sixty five!* To me, that's testament to three things: how far I had come in two years, how well I prepared, and how ridiculously long the race is. When I tried it the first time, I had only really been running for two years - and the improvement curve is steep at the beginning. I dabbled in many distances, and improved at each of them as I moved from novice to experienced.

I put up a little sheet of paper on my wall listing each distance, and my Personal Record at it. As time went on, I got that funny feeling of having a little secret that was pushing me, like innings passing at a no-hitter. It motivated me at every race, and it eventually even impacted which races I signed up for. My second iron-distance was another mark on the streak:

since I took up running four years earlier, I had PR'd every race.

The second time around, I decided not to just kick back after the race and binge-eat ice cream, but actually practice good recovery. After all, the race was one heck of a workout, and I came out stronger. But man, was I tired. When I attempted short runs, I was happy to meet up with my friends and tell race-stories, but my legs were heavy and slow. Under other circumstances, I would have backed off even more and kicked into off-season mode, but I still had another important race coming up: the New York City Marathon.

The NYC marathon is huge; it's epic. The front of the pack is dominated by the stuff of world records, the field is dotted with celebrities, and the course runs through five of the most famous boroughs in the world. My own participation came from good luck in the lottery - truly, it came from good marathon karma. On my way back from Athens the previous year, I had an overnight layover in New York the day of the marathon. With the strange westbound jet lag, I was wide awake at 2:30 a.m., and had enough time to catch a cab into the city, visit the famed race site, see the leaders, and even step foot into the hallowed finish chute in Central Park. Though I could have walked up to the deserted finish line on that early November morning, reverence stopped me: *you have to earn it.*

So, serendipitously I dropped my name in the hat, and got in. I got in to a full marathon that happened to be seven weeks after my season's September A-race triathlon. Training for New York was shadowed by Ironman, but nonetheless I turned around a quick recovery, got my legs back under myself as best I could, and felt generally ready. I was ready to have a good time and experience this quintessential race - but not sub-4-hour ready. Not faster than I'd ever run before. Not even faster than the marathon I'd just finished within the long-course triathlon.

It was clear that it was time to let go of my PR streak. *I'm gonna be free.*

Contemplating the Streak challenged me to think about

what I really value in running. It feels great to PR races and know that I've continued to improve. In my first four marathons, I took off 23 minutes, then 27 minutes, then *two* minutes, then *two* minutes again. The numbers converge as you get closer to your potential; the margins get slimmer. I came to realize that if I want to keep running and racing for the indefinite rest of my life, I'm simply not going to always continue to get faster. I'm optimistic that I still have plenty of room to improve toward my very best self, but I had to face it - my streak was impossible.

It became oppressive, too. I found that with each year, I'd add more asterisks next to race results. When I ran a race with a friend, with the intention of pacing that friend or just keeping them on track at a pace far off my own best, that didn't count. Asterisks started to appear in my training log, with entries like "*training run for so-and-so, ran with him" or "*coached team, hung back." One cold slushy winter day I didn't put on my chip for a local fundraiser 10k. I opted out of other perfectly fun races on days I didn't feel like I had the legs for my personal best.

It felt akin to the bogus excuse that keeps too many people from attempting their goals: *if I can't be perfect, I don't want to even try it.* Often, the only thing in the way turns out to be fictitious, fabricated by the mind. Didn't my own training credo tell me to challenge this kind of roadblock to defining *actual* success? The Streak had developed a life of its own, replacing motivation with resentment.

There are some streaks worth keeping: fidelity, truth to one's self, compassion. Heck, even safe driving. But PR'ing every race, ever? *Come on, Dano.* I'm not even in it for the times. So, I asked myself: why even bother with asterisks at all? Why not run races for what they are: some hard, some easy, some fast, some slow? Make PR'ing a goal at some races, and at some others, *fuhgettaboutit!*

I could have kept up the streak for its own sake, but I'd have had to intentionally walk away from good opportunities, just to keep it alive. Or I'd have had to put training before other things that are important to me, and training as part of a healthy lifestyle would fall out of balance. I wasn't about to walk away from the cosmos telling me it was time to run the New York City Marathon just to maintain an inconsequential personal statistic.

I wanted to see the Big Apple from inside the field of 50,000 runners, and take in the unique experience it had to offer. I wanted to stop and take pictures. I wanted to use walk intervals so that my quads didn't burn out, and see if I couldn't still run a smart, healthy race with a solid negative-split and a smiling finish in spite of an abbreviated training schedule. Lamb-o, the pocked-sized world-traveling lamb who makes little documentary films for my nieces, wanted to run with me. So I bid farewell to the first four years of running: the name of the game was about to change. This marathon was going to be just for fun, just like they're supposed to be. I wanted to be a part of it.

NEW YORK CITY - AND BEYOND

I'd sum up the New York City Marathon as *a 26.2-mile victory lap*. I've done some large, monumental, and interesting races, but indeed, New York City is truly a unique experience. I've gotten energy from fans in the past, but never at this magnitude. I've even lived near New York city, but never saw its beating heart quite like this.

It was the right day to leave concerns for timing behind. In spite of still-tired legs from the Ironman just 7 weeks prior, and a day of expo-visiting and whirlwind-sightseeing the day before, I drew on my race knowledge to put together the physical and emotional strength I needed to get through the marathon itself - for the sake of taking in all that New York offered me along the way.

Race morning began early on the upper west side at a friend's apartment, at 3:40 - with an extra hour thanks to Daylight Savings Time. The silent street and deserted subway station greeted me, ahead of my schedule but still barely able to keep from running. I took the A-train, then the downtown 1 train to South Ferry. At that point, other runners were filling up the subway car, and I chatted with four 20-somethings just leaving a bar and heading home. They kept referring to the marathon as "tomorrow," and I noted, "the marathon is *today!*" I caught the 5:30 a.m. ferry to Staten Island. Although it seemed ridiculously early considering my 10:10 a.m. start time, the place quickly became packed with thousands of runners making their way to the starting corrals.

Rounding out race-morning transportation was a bus from the ferry to the starting village, where I settled in for four hours of waiting until the start. Frost covered the ground as runners streamed in, wearing all sorts of bags and giveaway clothes. Coffee, bagels, bars, tea, and water rounded out my generous breakfast platter as I took a seat and struck up a conversation with a fellow runner, who turned out to be from Minnesota - and who, like me, had also spent the previous day touring the city. I passed the time chatting, waiting in the bathroom line, refilling my coffee… waiting in the bathroom line, and being happy to be there.

New York did give me one PR, for being my stickiest race to-date. I inadvertently pierced one of my gels before even starting, which oozed onto my belt, shirt, gloves, and shorts, and generally stayed with me the entire day. Shortly after the race began, I decided that my number bib was too high, and for some unknown reason decided to move it while running, which of course resulted in stabbing myself with the pin and bleeding. Later in the race, the huge volume of discarded cups and gel packs made each water station a wet mess of paper pulp, followed by the rip-rip-rip of sticky shoes glued to the asphalt with every step, and strange pulpy-dots on the back of runners' calves.

From the starting line in Staten Island, with "New York, New York" blaring, choppers overhead thumping, and the announcer shouting, the country's biggest marathon begins and runners climb up and over the Verrazano Narrows by way of the longest-spanning bridge in the Americas. Frankly, the running was somewhat incidental for me. I paid little attention to my pace throughout the whole day besides trying to keep it "easy." When I felt inclined to stop for a photo, I did; slap hi-fives and say hello - absolutely. When one group of people shouted "Go Team," I swerved over to shake an outstretched hand, the owner of whom looked me in the eye and exclaimed, "Thank you, Team In Training, you saved my life!"

As soon as we came off the bridge, fans greeted runners with signs saying "welcome to Brooklyn." New York had rolled out the red carpet for us. This was the focus of my race: the people, the languages spoken, and the flags flown by runners and spectators alike. When I was in Greece the year before, it was easy for me to feel good about the spirit of international hospitality and community because it was so specific, and somehow distant. But as I ran through New York's neighborhoods, I challenged myself to consider the subtle prejudices that I carry for fellow Americans with whom I interact more frequently - and let them go in favor of the hospitality and community I was experiencing right here at "home." The great American melting pot stood along the street in millions, singing and dancing, encouraging me and the international running community. Somewhere near mile 2, I thought: I hope this is the way New York felt on that fateful September day when all the rest of the world was encouraging them.

I'm sure I expended extra energy smiling and waving and jumping up onto barriers to take pictures. My eye muscles were exhausted from scanning the crowds - and actually seeing a handful of friends who had casually said "I'll watch for you." It pays to wear bright purple; it pays to look around. I took systematic walk breaks through the water stations and up the hills to refresh myself.

The Streak was broken, and thank goodness. If it had still been hanging over my head, my pace would have been my focus, and falling behind a fabricated number would have introduced a word I don't associate with this triumphant marathon: *failure*. Quite the contrary: giving myself the freedom to experience the race for other reasons took judgment out of the picture. I noticed the interesting differences between my body, which was really very sore and tired, and my mind, which was alert and very happy with the day. It became clear that feeling happy isn't limited to those times when you feel physically good.

The marathon showed me its might and - as usual - became harder as the miles went on. My residual fatigue probably contributed even more in the late miles, which seemed particularly long. Did you know that 5th Avenue isn't really flat? I did battle with the rolling hills in the last 10k. On the other hand, I found myself speeding up a bit, from the intentionally "easy" pace I held, to what was perhaps my more "natural" pace, in spite of being sore and tired. The final miles brought the quintessential marathon paradox (*maradox?*): wanting to stay out on the course to take it all in, and at the same time wanting it to all be over.

But then, there it was: the finish line. *Of the New York City Marathon.* The medal was big, golden, and heavy; I put it on and wore it proudly. After I showered, I put it back on. At dinner, the waiter at a little Mexican joint way up on 186th Street saw it, shook my hand, then brought out a round of drinks for the table, with the house's compliments and congratulations.

Monday morning we headed into the city for a little sightseeing before the afternoon flight home, and I was reluctant: should I wear my medal again? I decided yes, I should, and proudly strolled slowly through the likes of Times Square and Rockefeller Plaza, flashing big smiles and knowing thumbs-ups to hundreds of other medal-wearing slow-walkers out on the street. Some sported cameras and toured the city while others used their medals to adorn sharp suits on their way to the office.

I'm glad I set my pace to try to comprehend this enormous race rather than rush it. I'm glad my heart was open to experiencing humanity in a refreshing way. It's OK in those late miles to want it to all be over, because indeed, the race doesn't end at the finish line, it goes on. For perpetuity, I even got published in the New York Times. (My name, anyway). The thrill of victory doesn't fade, and I will never forget the feeling of running the 26.2-mile victory lap.

TRI THERAPY

If it were all about the numbers, another version of this book could make a fascinating research paper. I'd delve into statistics of who shows up at the races - their ages, jobs, relationships, economics. Their spending in tons of carbon fiber, compared to troubling trends in the nation's collective weight. I'd figure out who they are. I'd survey the field and find out why they show up, and what makes them tick. But I'm just a guy writing down the things I've noticed, and the changes I've seen in myself. Along the way, I've shared the road with a lot of others, and though the examples I share are anecdotal, I suspect research would only confirm the assessment I've already made.

Many of my tri-friends are people who already appear to have a full plate: medical and veterinary students, professionals, parents. These avocations are strong, but can also be overwhelming. They're linked to external demands and expectations, and the stresses that come along. Many come to the sport with a charitable objective - dealing with challenges that they didn't choose - and they seek some kind of symbolism or redemption. Some are looking to fill a hole: they show up with fresh wounds from change and loss, knowing only that they need to somehow rebuild. We're standing at the starting line.

Of course, the field will also contain seasoned veterans, hard-core old-school competitors, and professionals whose relationship with the sport is more urgently connected to their livelihood. It's likely that some will be entirely and blindly focused on the clock and their finish position. And like anyone who dares articulate his credo, I recognize that I will share the road with people who think that this text is a bunch of philosophical hogwash. I briefly consider whether this challenging sport once restricted to hard-bodied stoics is being overrun by social misfits and theater people looking for a new expression of themselves. Nevertheless, we each are seeking something.

Perhaps the real commonality of who we are is that we are all looking for something about who we are. We're curious about what happens when we push our own limits, but are reassured by the notion that a "failure" here is likely to be far more forgiving than in other settings. There's an order within training that invites us to experience a new level of confidence and control. There's a reasonably predictable justice of cause and effect that gives structure to our reinvention. This thing we call "training" can end up referring less to preparation for a race ahead of us, and more to breaking free of the tensions holding us back... from anything. It's a sacred sanctuary where we feed our bodies and souls the energy they need in order to thrive. It's therapy.

If we dive in with enough abandon to fully focus, new ways of seeing life will appear. There are fascinating nuggets of beauty in every life experience, however small, if you look for them. As I committed to my training efforts and inspected the lifestyle they promote, I developed a new appreciation for more facets of life. I paid closer attention to the world around me, especially its vast outdoor spaces. Racing challenges us to appreciate the complicated mechanisms that make up our living bodies, made more beautiful as we hone them and try to get more out of them. Life is taking in full breaths of air, feeling the sun's energy, and appreciating a substance as fundamental as water as we move through it. This is life on earth - real life.

Racing might seem like a break from "ordinary" life, but inside its realm, we have the chance to feel intensely alive. Its energy cannot be contained, and begins permeating everything else - begging us to feel more alive through all the moments of life. And eventually, all of life starts to shift, so that indeed *all* of it is a break - from what used to be "ordinary." Fears and woes that used to appear insurmountable are relinquished to a time gone by.

Something happened that inspired each of us to start the journey, and regardless of the specific circumstances from which we began, we each have the opportunity to let it impact us. The extent to which the process shapes us comes directly from how malleable we are ready to let ourselves become. To not know the final outcome is to be vulnerable, but we are reassured by knowing that simply looking - looking diligently - for a way to define ourselves will be a gratifying end in itself. My biggest races have made lasting changes in my life not because I was perfect, but because I was committed.

Having a good time with the sport supersedes winning; enjoying the things we choose for leisure allows those activities to relieve our tension. Just as getting faster comes from hard work, gaining happiness comes from practicing joy. Taking positive elements of the same leisure into everything else gives it a curative power that transcends age or time or physical fitness. The best we can aim to achieve is learning to live inside of each of life's moments, and finding victories everywhere, in whatever way we might think of them.

When I first took up running, I don't think I set out to define "what is the meaning of life?" More frequently I thought "when will this start to feel *good*?" But eventually, it did start to feel good, and I did indeed start to question the new ways in which I defined myself. I'm no longer a person defined by my day-job or my relationships, who happens to do triathlon; I'm a triathlete whose life includes many facets that I can achieve because I am strong. You might catch me stretching in the break room or in line at the grocery store, but you might never notice that beneath the veneer of business pants are green knee-high compression socks. You might never discover this thing that motivates me. But I hope you do.

FOR PERPETUITY

Unlike a race, which has a finish line, course marshals and referees, and a big clock that stops after a certain point, writing does not. I type these words just after my five-year anniversary with triathlon, having completed the same fun local race as I did to kick off the whole tri-journey. Of course, I'm different now in some ways, and just the same in others. There isn't a distinct lifetime goal that I will achieve - some immaculate finish line that will mark the end of my athletic career - like the end of any one race and all the benchmarks it brings. Similarly, many times I have experienced something that said to me "this, Dano, is how you will wrap up your book." Each time, that conclusion lasted for a while but was superseded... until the end of The Streak in New York. That ending had more significance than other beginnings: if racing is going to enhance my life, it will have to do so in a sustainable way.

After spending a day traveling 140.6 miles, a title is bestowed: "You are an Ironman." It's not something that has been finished - it's something that you *are*. With all the rights and responsibilities therein. When I am an Ironman in the permanent sense, people seem to somehow believe that I am also prepared to complete an iron-distance triathlon at any given time, or any combination of its parts (like, say, a marathon.) This may be true for some athletes who constantly train and maintain a super-high level of fitness, but I know that I would need to put in a lot of seriously focused training to complete that distance again. For me, the perpetual title defines something that remains inside me, thanks to the way I got there.

There are some parts to the perpetual "Ironman" title that do indeed persist regardless of current race-readiness. Those parts of the race for which I trained mentally and spiritually as much as physically seem to be permanently ready. When I spent an entire year gaining an appreciation for the water, cultivating peace in my mind in the midst of darkness or waves or splashing bubbles, I effectively came to a definitive conclusion about the water. That is, my arms get tired quicker if they're not exercised regularly, or I may not be able to swim as far in one go, but I am comfortable in the water. I can survive in it. I respect it as a challenging and dangerous medium, but it's a realm I know I can enjoy.

When training schedules are based on goals, and the goals are defined by concepts, the training not only creates strength in a sport, it creates competence and confidence in those concepts that last beyond the period of training. One swim session might have included instructions like "ladder to 250 by 50's," which was one element of the larger goal of "build up to swimming 4,000 yards continuously." But overriding all of these was my own top goals of becoming comfortable in the water and getting balanced, which guided all of my decisions. In spring, the offseason's rust may hold me back from the speed or endurance I once knew, but deeper skills remain. The most fundamental concepts I trained toward became a part of me, and have stuck. I suspect that even if I were to put the sport down for a while, I'd be pretty successful in picking it back up.

As a matter of fact, I think it has to be set down and backed off from time to time. I'm thankful for the drastically-different seasons in Wisconsin because they encourage me to frequently change my routines, re-evaluate my priorities, and stay fresh. I'm thankful for avoiding burnout with one of the sport's great blessings: the off-season. I'm thankful for low-volume training weeks mixed in with high-volume ones. If the volume is high all the time, life becomes unsustainable. With every mountaintop, there are valleys; many of them are green and lush.

Considering my own journey to becoming a leader, if someone else hadn't backed off, I might not have had the chance to become a coach. I wonder who else might be beginning the meaningful journey that I once did, who might I make room for by stepping aside from time to time? Only by listening will I find out. One of the joys of racing is the shared course: my participation and skill level does not impinge on the opportunities of anyone else. Many roles are needed within any community to help it thrive - a combination of participants and leaders and motivators at various levels - and as the years go on, I watch for the kinds of roles I am best at playing.

In July of my fifth summer of triathlon, I found myself in uniform and prepared to race my second half-iron-distance tri in Door County. I stood on a platform next to the race director, facing Old Glory, and offered up the Star-Spangled banner to a field of 1,000. I didn't get paid, or get special consideration for my finish time. I volunteered, because it was something I had to offer that I thought would enhance the race's atmosphere. Perhaps it made some athletes' day at the race even faster, but I do not consider this a detriment to my own race-outcome. I'm sure my impression of "patriotism" is different than others', but I trust that the fundamentals symbolized by this song are good and true. The race community benefits from a National Anthem singer just as it needs the non-racing community members to volunteer at the water stops. Some days you race, some days you make races happen; sometimes you can do both.

The "rest of our lives" - come Monday morning after race day - also needs us. It needs "runners" and "triathletes." It needs a different form of what we take away from the races, translated into the day-to-day. My workplace, like many in America, needs role models for healthy habits, in some way that is approachable to its members. It doesn't need me to be a superstar long-course finisher, it needs a down-to-earth companion and guide. When the idea arose to offer a community-supported agriculture program at my office, I volunteered to help run it, because I know what benefits can come from healthy eating. When you go home from your race, ask yourself not just how much more fit you have become, but how you might turn your investment in yourself into an inspiration and motivation for others.

I find myself searching: what does it mean to be this "athlete" I have become? It doesn't mean being spiteful, alienating others, or defeating someone else. Rather, it means addressing my own limiters on the way to being the best self that I can be. The best self that I can offer, as much as it might help others also achieve their best selves. I recently caught myself whining over something trite, and asked myself, "what good is being an Ironman if you're going to be whiny?" Indeed, the practice is ongoing - the outcome is not a race, but a way of living.

The title "Ironman" has been important to my healthy lifestyle, because it keeps me accountable to sticking with my own level of fitness. I like the perception that I am strong because of the thing I earned, and do indeed want to remain strong. It motivates me to keep up some kind of regular "training," whether or not a specific race is coming up. Some friends choose to pursue the long course and ask me for advice because I have finished it. I want to share and write about my experiences - but not only would I feel hypocritical saying them if I were a lazy bum, no one would believe me. I feel better about myself when I am this thing I have earned, I feel committed to its permanent title. The thing perpetuates itself.

***

The day after Ironman Wisconsin, as the family casually

enjoyed the mild September day together, my mom said to me, "I didn't want to say this before, but I always thought that as you expend energy, you seem to have *more and more* energy." Yes, I think she's absolutely right. Mom is always right. In spite of the sun setting, I usually don't want to come in from a project that's not yet finished. It's so much easier to keep going, just a little more, when I know the end is just ahead.

My perspective changes when I am well into something - when I have committed to it and am moving confidently toward its finish. When I'm all in, I'm able to say, over and over, "just one more..." When times get hard, this perseverance keeps me going; conditions change and hard situations do end. It's no wonder that endurance sports are a good match for me, that something even as long as a 140.6-mile triathlon wouldn't beat me down, it would bring me up.

The finish chute is disassembled and moved on to the next race somewhere else. The roads are reopened. The first day after, my body is very sore and it's slow going. Down stairs is the toughest part - the trick is to go down backwards. Change your perspective. I recover by sleeping extra, eating extra, and seeking to regain a "normal" feeling.

By Wednesday, the soreness has mostly worn off, and I begin to wonder what "normal" is, anyway. The extra time, once occupied with training, gives moments of pause: "wow, what will I do now?" *Maybe I should write a book.* "When will I see my running buddies again?" By Thursday, I feel like something is missing, and begin to wonder: "maybe I should do another one."

See you at the races.
Cheers,
Dano

THE END

Made in the USA
Lexington, KY
21 October 2013